Using Color in Your Art!

Choosing Colors for Impact & Pizzazz

Sandi Henry

Illustrations by Sarah Rakitin

(A WILLIAMSON *KIDS CAN!*® BOOK)

WILLIAMSON BOOKS
NASHVILLE, TENNESSEE

ISBN 0-8249-6754-2 (paper)
ISBN 0-8249-6772-0 (case)

Library of Congress Cataloging-in-Publication Data

Henry, Sandi, 1951–
    Using color in your art! : choosing colors for impact & pizzazz / Sandi Henry : illustrations by Sarah Rakitin.
            p. cm.
    "A Williamson kids can! book."
    Includes index.
    (alk. paper)
    1.   Color in art—Juvenile literature. 2.   Art—Study and teaching (Elementary)—Activity programs.   I. Rakitin, Sarah. II. Title.

    N7432.7.H46 2005
    372.5—dc22
                    2005002762

Kids Can!® series editor: **Susan Williamson**
Project editor: **Vicky Congdon**
Interior design: **Sydney Wright**
Interior illustrations: **Sarah Rakitin**
Cover design and illustrations: **Michael Kline**

Published by Williamson Books
An imprint of Ideals Publications
A division of Guideposts
800-586-2572

Printed in ITALY by L.E.G.O. S.p.a. All rights reserved.
10 9 8 7 6 5 4 3 2 1

Kids Can!®, Little Hands®, Quick Starts for Kids!®, Kaleidoscope Kids®, and Tales Alive!® are registered trademarks of Ideals Publications, a division of Guideposts.

Good Times™, Quick Starts Tips!™, Quick Starts Jump-Starts™, and You Can Do It!™ are trademarks of Ideals Publications, a division of Guideposts.

Permissions

page 14: Photograph by David Heald © The Solomon R. Guggenheim Foundation, New York

page 30: Photograph © The Art Institute of Chicago. All rights reserved.

page 88: © 2005 Artists Rights Society (ARS), New York/ADAGP, Paris; Photograph by David Heald © The Solomon R. Guggenheim Foundation, New York

page 102: © 2005 Artists Rights Society (ARS), New York/VG Bild-Kunst, Bonn; Photograph by David Heald © The Solomon R. Guggenheim Foundation, New York

page 110: © 2005 The Georgia O'Keeffe Foundation/Artists Rights Society (ARS), New York; Photo: Katherine Wetzel, © Virginia Museum of Fine Arts

Permission is granted by the following artists to reproduce their work in this book:

Through the Artist's Eyes: Tera Belk, Jessika Henry, William Lawrence, Joe Miller, Pamela Torres, Janet Walsh.

Student Art: Angel Assad, Ayla Assad, Zia Assad, Danielle Bullock, Emily Bullock, Audrey Burton, Emily Cheshier, Derek Cook, Meghan Cook, Candice Corbin, Mariah Corbin, Cody Critcher, Alex Derrick, Jenna Derrick, Ben Dodson, Sallie Dowell, Kelsey Hall, Matthew Hall, Brent Levi Hammer, Laura Henry, Isaac Hodges, Kaitlin Horne, Jessica Kilkelly, Makala Matthews, Trey McNeil, Brian Miller, Julia Padgett, Noah Padgett, Hillary Prevost, Tom Prevost, Becky Price, Tyler Prosch, Josh Roberts, Tim Roberts, Jordan Thomas, Willow Warner, Jasa Woods, Jenna Woods, Colleen Whittington, Hannah Whittington.

Dedication

In memory of my father, Rex Inman, who always believed in me.

Acknowledgments

My thanks and appreciation to my husband, Terry, for sharing his expertise in all computer-related aspects of preparing the manuscript.

Special thanks to all the young artists who contributed the wonderful artwork in this book. Deepest appreciation to Jessika Henry, Janet Walsh, Joe Miller, Pamela Torres, Tera Belk, and Skip Lawrence, who provided their original works of art for the book.

Thanks to Susan Williamson for believing in this book and for putting together a great team to make it happen. Thanks to Vicky Congdon for her editorial skill in the revision of the text, to Sarah Rakitin and Sydney Wright for the illustrations and design, and to Michael Kline for the cover design.

My thanks to God, the source of all color.

Contents

Beautiful Bouquet,
page 40
Tom, age 10

Moonlit Night,
page 86
Jasa, age 12

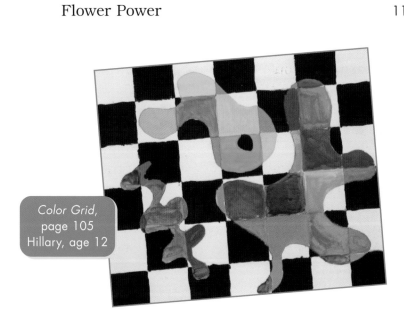

Color Grid,
page 105
Hillary, age 12

Creating with Color!

The famous painter Georgia O'Keeffe once said, "I can say things with color and shapes that there are no words for."

When you want a piece of art to pop off the page, what do you think about first? The colors, of course. When you want your artwork to express just how you feel, whether you're full of excitement or in a quiet mood, what do you carefully choose? Colors again. And whether you're creating a realistic-looking scene or a purely imaginative design, what's a key part of the overall impression? You guessed it, the colors.

Without a doubt, color is one of the most striking elements in a piece of art. In most paintings, for example, it's the aspect we respond to first, which is why I've chosen paint as the *medium* (material) for the color explorations in this book. Once you understand how colors are related, you'll see which ones work well together, and you'll know just why some colors seem to jump off the page while others blend in with the colors around them. You'll see how the students in my art classes applied those colors and their relationships to their artwork. You'll also meet all kinds of artists, both famous painters from the past and living artists of today, and discover how they used color to achieve certain effects in their artwork. But most of all, you'll have fun applying all these "colorful" ideas to create your own art that uses color in an effective way.

Color has a language of its own. Learn to let the colors in your art speak for you!

Sandi Henry

Getting Started

All you really need to start creating with color is paint, paper, and a paintbrush. I've included some recommendations here that will make your art explorations more rewarding and will ensure that all your paintings look their best! These supplies can be purchased at most art supply stores (or see RESOURCES, page 125).

Before starting any art project, always protect your work surface with old newspaper. It makes cleanup very easy, too. Wear an old shirt to protect your clothes from paint.

Ice Cream Sundae, Makala, age 8

Paint

Tempera paint is a water-based paint that is *opaque* (you can't see through it). It comes in a powder form that you mix with water or in liquid form. I recommend the liquid variety. Look for a "premium grade" tempera. It has an acrylic medium added to it to keep it from cracking.

Liquid tempera paint comes in a wide range of individual colors. All you need for these art projects are the primary colors (use magenta, yellow, and turquoise; see page 9) and the secondary colors (orange, green, and violet), along with black and white.

Watercolor paint is a water-based paint that's *transparent* (you can see through it). When you add water to the dry cake of color in your paint box, it dissolves into a liquid that you can paint with. A box of eight watercolor paints is perfect for the activities in this book.

Illustrations & Icons

The activities in this book are illustrated with paintings by my art students. Their artwork is meant only to guide you, and I encourage you to apply the color concepts to create your *own* pieces of art. To that end, the step-by-step illustrations sometimes show different colors or shapes than the finished art — there is no one "correct" way to complete any of these projects!

The level of difficulty is identified with these icons:

These simple activities require a minimum of materials and use basic art techniques. Perfect for beginning students.

These activities offer a medium challenge level. They work well with students in second to fourth grades.

These activities are the most challenging. They introduce slightly more advanced concepts and sometimes require detailed brushwork or a sense of perspective. For students in fifth, sixth, and seventh grades.

🎨 Paintbrushes

Camel's hair paintbrushes have soft bristles and are good for both tempera and watercolor paints. They don't have to be expensive and with the proper care, they'll last a long time.

I recommend owning several brushes in different sizes. *Flat-ended brushes* give you a wide brushstroke. They can be used for watercolor washes (page 39) or for filling in a large area of paint. *Round-ended brushes* are numbered according to thickness. A basic round number 6 brush is a good choice for most watercolor projects. A number 4 works well for detail painting.

🎨 Paper

Paper comes in different thicknesses, indicated by a weight. White *vellum paper*, 60 lb or heavier, is a good choice for tempera paints.

Watercolor paints look their best on watercolor paper or an absorbent white paper. Look for a weight of 90 lbs or heavier. Thicker paper won't wrinkle as much when you paint on it.

Color Dance,
page 89
Julia, age 10

All Great Artists Know to . . .

Keep their paint colors clean! Taking a minute to clean your brush between colors can make a huge difference between getting clear, clean paint colors on your paper and getting a murky mess. When you are ready to switch to a new color, wash the brush by gently swishing it in the bottom of the water container. Then wipe it on a paper towel to remove excess water. Change the water as needed.

Take care of their brushes! When you're finished painting, always clean your brushes with warm water and mild dish detergent and place them on a paper towel to dry. Store them in a container with the bristles pointing *up.*

Avoid wrinkles! Before you start a watercolor project, tape the corners of the paper to a large piece of cardboard to keep it from wrinkling when you apply the paint. Carefully remove the tape after the picture is completely dry.

Primary Colors

Red, yellow, and blue are the **primary colors**.

Primary means "first," so think of these three as the first colors. Each one is a pure color that is not created by mixing other colors together. What's more, these three colors are the ones you mix to make all the others!

Look at the position of these colors on the right. This shape is a handy way to picture the primaries — an equal distance apart from each other and no color coming first or last.

Primary colors are bright and bold, and they contrast the most strongly with each other because each one is pure, with no other color mixed in. So they really stand out when you use them in your artwork!

Reds & Blues:

Getting Them Right

Wait a minute, you say. As you already know, there are lots of different blues, for example, from deep royal blue to pale blue. So what's "primary blue"? Picture the color of a clear blue sky on a beautiful sunny day. That's very close to primary blue.

It's important to make sure that the blue and red paints you're using match primary blue and primary red. That way, when you mix those primary colors together to make new colors, they will also be accurate. In tempera paints, primary blue is actually closer to turquoise, and primary red is closest to magenta.

Sallie's Cardinal
Sallie, age 9

See how the primary colors make a simple but striking picture?

Color Wise
The Science Behind the Art

Have you ever wondered why things that look colorful in the day appear gray or black when the sun goes down? That's because we can only see color when there is light.

Sunlight appears kind of colorless, but it is actually made up of bands of color called *wavelengths*. Some of the bands are long, some are short, so they travel to our eyes at different speeds, each one representing a different color. Together, these seven colors — red, orange, yellow, green, blue, indigo, and violet — are called the *color spectrum*.

When we see a rainbow, we're seeing the color spectrum. The sunlight passes through the raindrops in the air, and they act as tiny prisms that separate the sunlight into the different bands of color.

Pattern Painting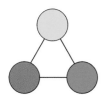

It's easy to create a pattern — you just repeat lines, colors, and shapes. And the primary colors — red, yellow, and blue — are perfect for creating striking patterns because they are bright and bold and contrast well next to each other. So pick a few favorite shapes or markings like hearts, ovals, X's, stars, or wiggly lines, and use them over and over in an interesting way.

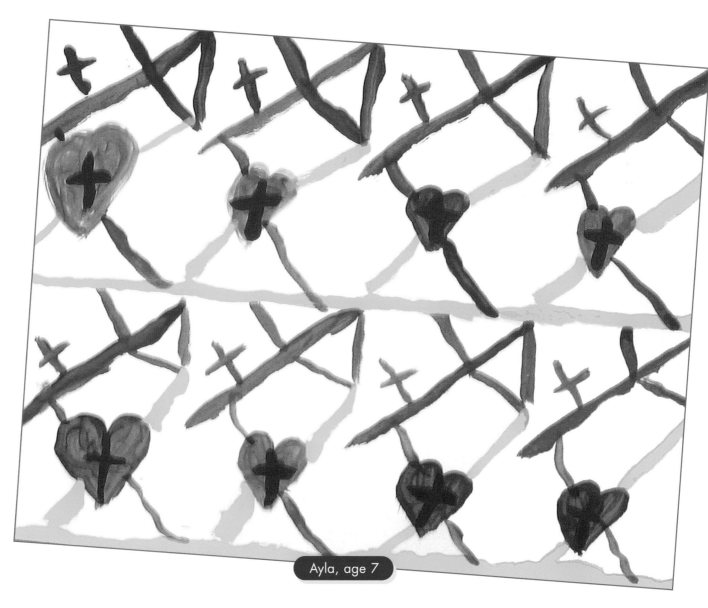

Ayla, age 7

What you need

Old newspaper to protect your work surface

Good-quality white paper
(9" x 12"/22.5 x 30 cm)

Tempera paints in red, yellow, and blue

Paintbrush

Container of water and paper towel to
clean paintbrush between colors

Create it with color!

1 Fold your paper as shown. Then unfold it.
You will have eight rectangles.

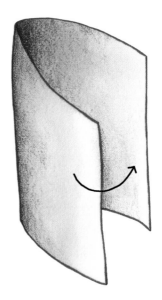

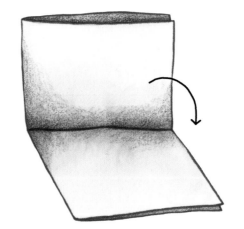

❷ Choose one primary color. Paint a line or shape in the first rectangle. Repeat that mark in each remaining rectangle. Take care to place the mark in the same place in each rectangle.

❸ Choose another primary color of paint. Make a different mark in each rectangle.

❹ Use the remaining primary color to make a similar mark in each rectangle. Add to your pattern by making additional repeating marks in each rectangle, if you like.

Pattern Hunt

Look for patterns all around your house. Check out rugs, wallpaper, tile floors, and especially right in your own closet! What do you particularly like about the patterns that are your favorites? Do any of them use the primary colors?

Meet the Masters!

Using Color in Art Then

The Dutch painter **Piet Mondrian** (PEE-et mohn-DREE-ahn) began his career painting landscapes and scenes from nature. But those aren't the paintings for which he is famous. During a trip to Paris in 1911, Mondrian was inspired by the work of several abstract artists. Mondrian began to paint abstract images (page 16), using straight lines to create squares and rectangles and filling in only certain shapes with primary colors.

Another painter once said of Mondrian that he couldn't bear to see anything disordered or untidy. It even upset him to see a dinner table that wasn't set with perfect symmetry! Can you see that love of order and a careful use of color to create a feeling of balance in this painting?

Piet Mondrian
Tableau 2, 1922
Oil on canvas; 21$^7/_8$ x 21$^1/_8$ inches (55.6 x 53.4 cm); 51.1309
Solomon R. Guggenheim Museum, New York

Primary-Color Pattern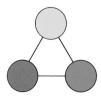

Combine horizontal and vertical lines with the primary colors to create an abstract painting in the style of Piet Mondrian. He painted many paintings in this style, so why not try several, experimenting to create a harmony between the sizes of the shapes and the placement of the colors, just as Mondrian did?

Kaitlin, age 7

What you need

Old newspaper to protect your work surface

Black crayon

Good-quality white paper, 2

Ruler (optional)

Tempera paints in red, yellow, and blue

Paintbrush

Container of water and paper towel to clean paintbrush between colors

Create it with color!

❶ Use the black crayon to draw vertical and horizontal lines on your paper to create different-sized squares and rectangles as shown. Use the ruler if you want the lines perfectly straight.

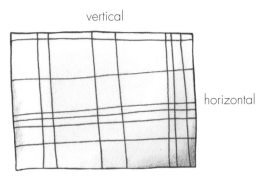
vertical
horizontal

❷ Look at the spaces created by the lines. Choose three or more shapes and fill them in with primary colors. Before you paint, think carefully about which spaces to fill in and which colors to use so the painting will make an impression on the viewer.

❸ On a new piece of paper, draw similar black lines. Now use the same colors in different rectangles. How is the effect different? Do you think your paintings look like ones by Piet Mondrian?

Abstract art

Abstract art is a style of art that doesn't attempt to create realistic images of things. Abstract artists take a recognizable subject, such as an animal or a landscape, and change it by using color in unusual ways or by rearranging the outline of the subject in an intriguing way. You can still see the subject, but it is changed, or *abstracted*. Or, abstract artists use geometric lines, shapes, and bright colors to create something that is purely a design.

Look at Mondrian's abstract painting shown on page 14, as well as other examples of abstract art on pages 75, 88, 102, and 119. Do you like these paintings? Or do you prefer a realistic image?

Hidden Tools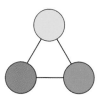

The bright, intense primary colors in this painting make your eyes dance over the images. Does it look to you as if the tools are moving?

Here's a technique for creating an abstract painting (page 16) using some common objects like tools. Just by adding a few lines, you can break up the images of the tools into abstract shapes. Then paint the shapes with primary colors.

Tim, age 12

What you need

Old newspaper to protect your work surface

Good-quality white paper
(12" x 18"/30 x 45 cm)

Pencil

Tools for tracing

Ruler

Tempera paints in red, yellow, and blue

Paintbrush

Container of water and paper towel to clean paintbrush between colors

Create it with color!

❶ On the paper, trace the outlines of four or five tools. Vary the positions and angles of the tools in relation to each other and even overlap some of them to create more interest.

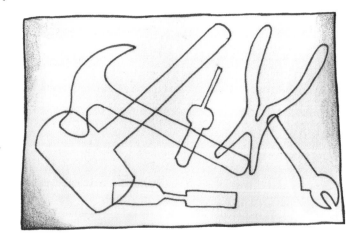

❷ Use the ruler to draw five lines that are not parallel to each other. Draw three in one direction and two in the other. See how the lines divide your picture into abstract shapes?

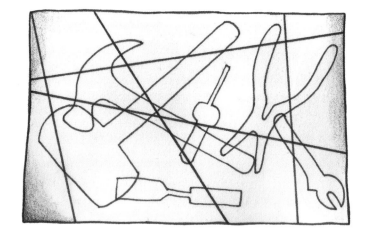

❸ Look at the shapes created by the lines (either dividing lines or outlines of the tools).

Think about which primary color to use in each shape for the most effect. Lightly pencil in the first letter of the color you want to use in that section.

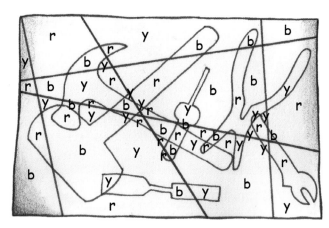

For contrast, be sure to use different colors for shapes that touch each other. When you're pleased with the arrangement of colors, erase the letter and paint, section by section.

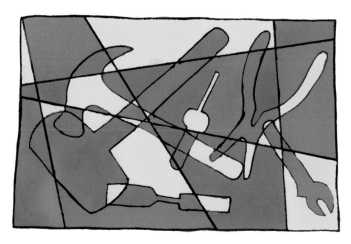

Meet the Masters!

Using Color in Art Then

The Russian artist **Vasily Kandinsky** (VAH-seh-lee kan-DIN-skee) used the primary colors for a striking effect in his abstract painting *Blue Mountain*. Take a look at this painting online at the website of the Solomon R. Guggenheim Museum in New York (RESOURCES, page 125). Kandinsky did use other colors in this painting, but what colors do you notice first? For more on Kandinsky, see page 88.

Secondary Colors

Were you surprised at what interesting artwork you could create using only the three primary colors (page 8)? Even so, you'd probably like a few more colors to work with. Easy! All you need to do is to mix equal amounts of the primaries in a few different ways.

This *second* set of colors — orange, green, and violet — is called the **secondary colors**. Just as with the primaries, think of these colors as "equals," as shown here.

Now you've got twice as many colors to paint with!

Rather than the pure colors of the primaries, the secondary colors are a mixture, so they are less intense. They're a good choice when you need a color that's good and strong but not quite as bold and bright as a primary.

primary + primary = secondary

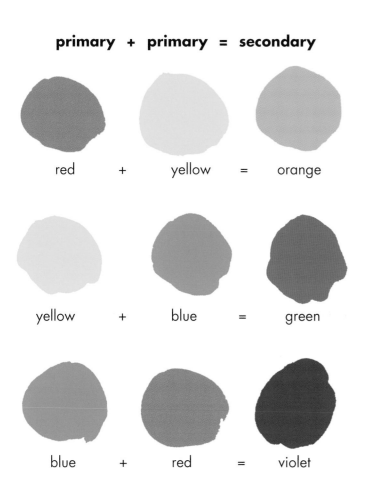

red + yellow = orange

yellow + blue = green

blue + red = violet

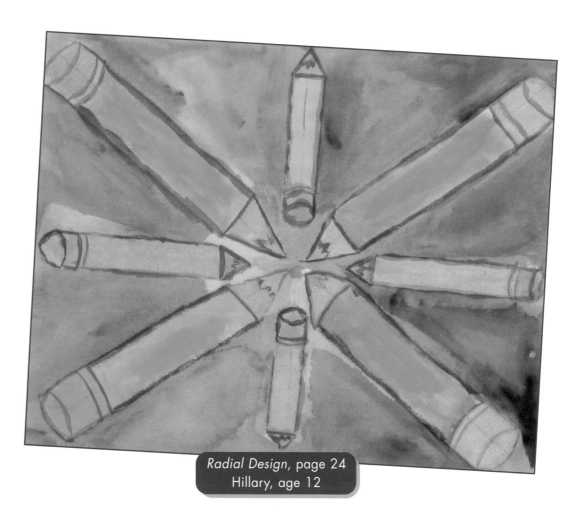

Radial Design, page 24
Hillary, age 12

String Painting

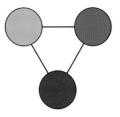

The primary colors mix together to create the secondary colors in a magical way when you pull paint-coated strings from between a folded piece of paper.

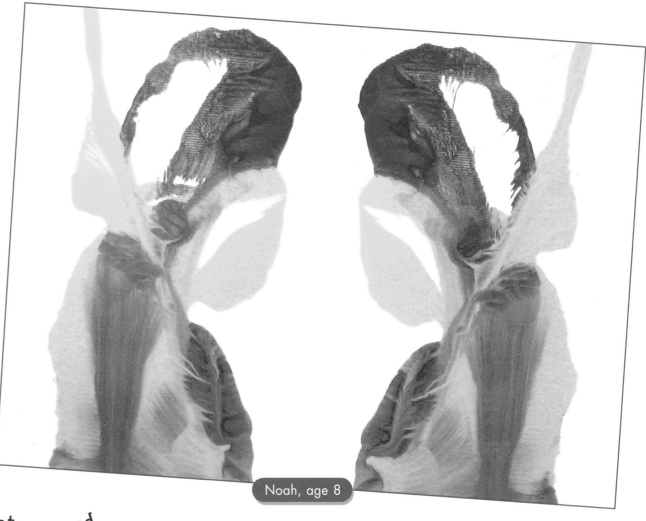

Noah, age 8

What you need

Old newspaper to protect your work surface

Paper towel

Tempera paints in red, yellow, and blue

Paper plates, 3

Good-quality white paper (6" x 9"/15 x 22.5 cm), 3

Lengths of string, 6

Create it with color!

❶ Pour a small amount of each paint onto a paper plate and thin it with a little water.

❷ Fold one sheet of paper in half, then open it. Dip one piece of string into the blue paint. Pull the string through your thumb and forefinger to remove excess paint. Arrange the string on half of the paper, allowing the string to loop a time or two. Let one end hang off the edge of the paper.

Repeat with another string and the yellow paint, making sure the end of the string hangs off the edge.

❸ Fold the paper over the strings. Apply pressure with one hand and with the other, pull the strings out from between the folded paper, one at a time.

❹ Unfold your paper to find two identical designs *plus* a surprise secondary green color! How did that happen?

❺ Repeat steps 2 through 4, experimenting with yellow and red paint to create the secondary color orange. Try it again with blue and red paint. What color did you create this time?

More Colorful Ideas!

Look on the both sides of the fold — what do you notice about your painting? You've made a mirror image. What do you see in your string painting? Add a few lines with a marker to develop your idea.

Radial Design

A *radial design* is a pattern that seems to *radiate* (move out) from the center to the outer edges. The illustrations here show how Laura created her design, but you can create your own, repeating the secondary colors of orange, green, and violet to make the viewer's eyes follow the radial pattern.

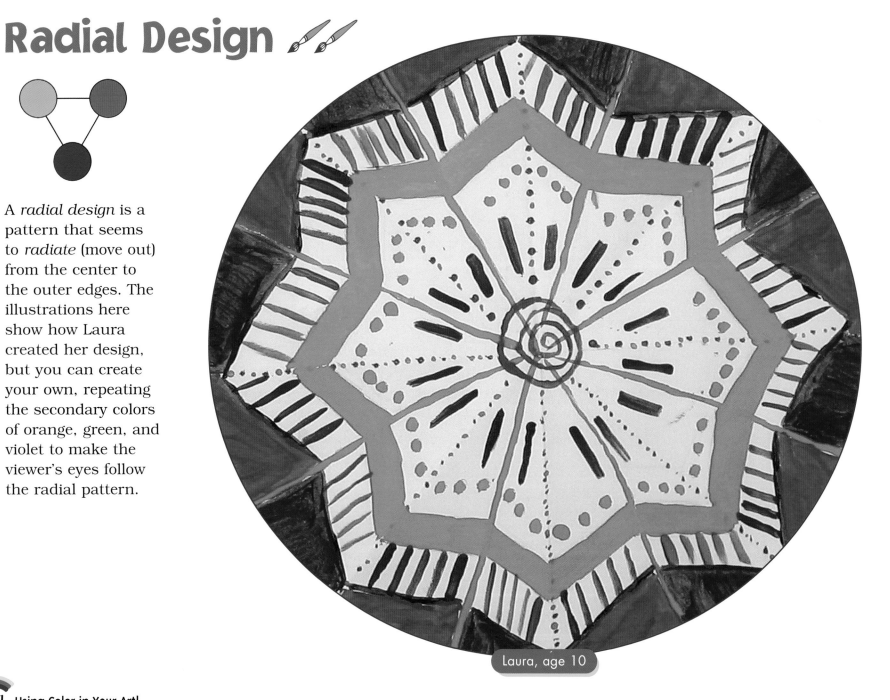

Laura, age 10

What you need

Old newspaper to protect your work surface

Pencil

Dinner plate (to trace around)

Good-quality white paper
(9" x 12"/22.5 x 30 cm)

Scissors

Tempera paints in orange, green,
and violet

Paintbrush

Container of water and paper towel to
clean paintbrush between colors

Create it with color!

❶ Trace around the plate to make a large circle on the
paper. Cut it out. Fold your circle three times as shown.
Open the circle to reveal eight pie shapes.

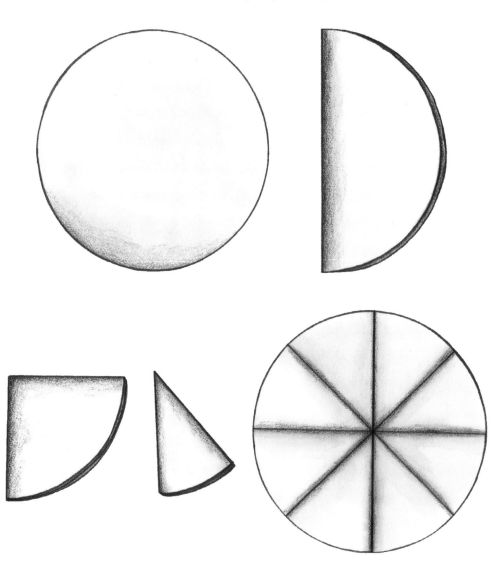

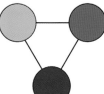

❷ Choose a secondary color and paint a line or shape in one section of your circle. Repeat the same shape in each pie-shaped section.

❸ Paint a line or shape in each section using a different secondary color.

Now use the remaining secondary color.

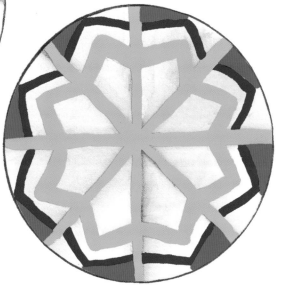

❹ Continue adding additional lines or shapes in each pie shape. Think carefully about how to repeat the three colors to make the design intriguing.

See how the vertical lines direct the viewer's eye from the center of the circle to the outer edge?

Using Color in Art Then

Marc Chagall (mark sha-GALL) was a French painter and stained glass artist born in Russia in 1887. His style of abstract art (page 16) reminds some people of images from dreams. His painting *Green Violinist* hangs in the Solomon R. Guggenheim Museum in New York; you can view it online at museum's website (RESOURCES, page 125). Notice how the secondary colors really pop out against the neutral background. Why do you think Chagall painted the violinist's face green?

Color Puzzle

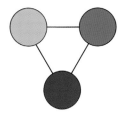

Overlap primary-colored triangles, squares, and circles to create areas of secondary colors. The result? A colorful puzzle design!

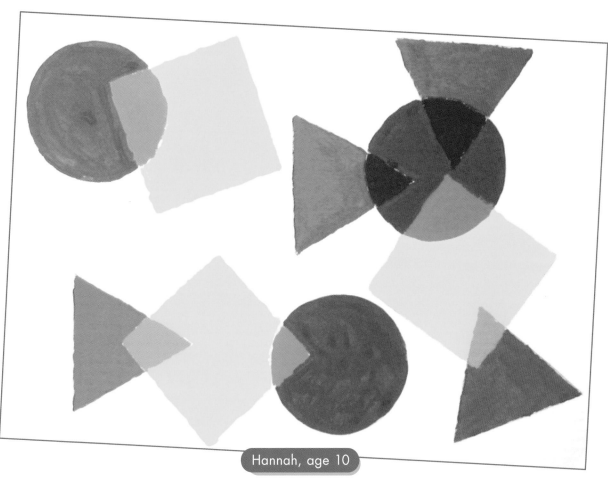

Hannah, age 10

What you need

Old newspaper to protect your work surface

Pencil

Circle, square, and triangle cut from cardboard (see MAKING A TEMPLATE, page 29)

Good-quality paper (12" x 18"/30 x 45 cm)

Tempera paints in red, yellow, and blue

Paintbrush

Paper plates for mixing paints

Container of water and paper towel to clean paintbrush between colors

Create it with color!

❶ Trace around each template three or four times onto your paper. Overlap the shapes in some areas.

❷ Paint all the squares yellow, the triangles red, and the circles blue. *Don't* paint the areas where shapes overlap.

❸ Mix yellow and blue to make green. Use it to paint each area where the yellow squares and the blue circles overlap.

❹ Mix blue and red together to make violet. Paint each area where blue circles overlap with red triangles with the violet.

❺ Mix red and yellow together to make orange. Paint the areas where the red triangles and the yellow squares overlap with the orange.

Making a Template

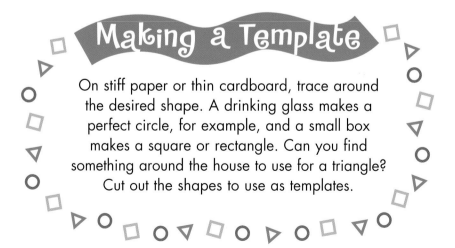

On stiff paper or thin cardboard, trace around the desired shape. A drinking glass makes a perfect circle, for example, and a small box makes a square or rectangle. Can you find something around the house to use for a triangle? Cut out the shapes to use as templates.

Georges Seurat (sir-RAH), a French artist who lived and painted in the late 1800s, created an unusual style of painting called *pointillism*. Seurat used tiny dots, or points, of color to create his images. If you were standing in front of the Seurat painting shown here, you would see that the people as well as the scenery are all made of dots of pure color. This huge painting, a scene of a park in Paris on a sunny afternoon, is Seurat's most famous work.

Georges Seurat
French, 1859–1891
A Sunday on La Grande Jatte
1884–86

Oil on canvas
81³/4 x 121¹/4 inches (207.5 x 308.1 cm)
Helen Birch Bartlett Memorial Collection
Reproduction, The Art Institute of Chicago

Color Dot Design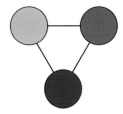

Try painting in the pointillism style of Georges Seurat. Create the secondary colors *and* an intriguing image at the same time by painting dots of two primary colors right next to each other.

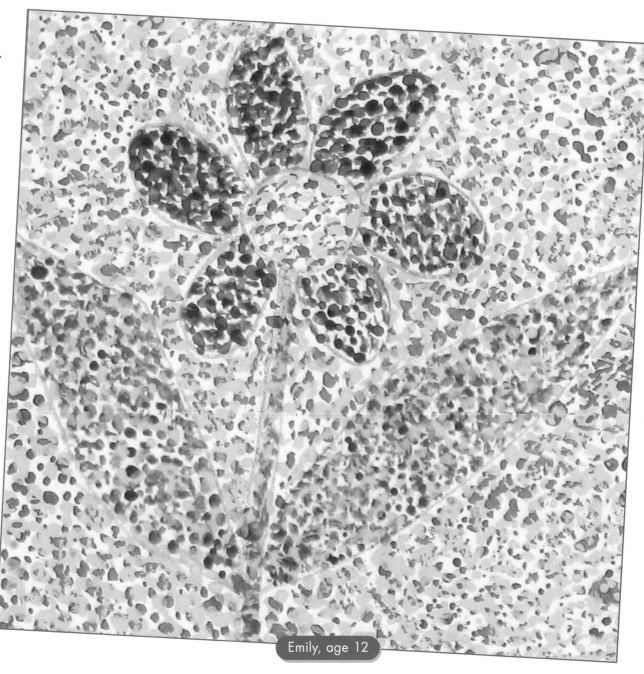

Emily, age 12

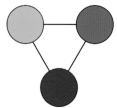

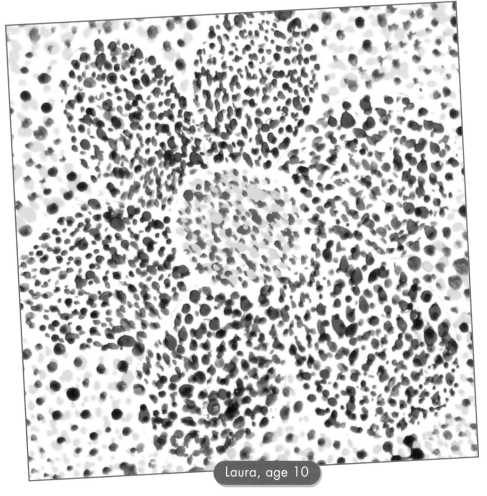

Laura, age 10

What you need

Old newspaper to protect your work surface

Pencil

Good-quality white paper
(4" x 4"/10 x 10 cm)

Tempera paints in red, yellow, and blue

Paintbrush with a fine point

Container of water and paper towel to
clean paintbrush between colors

Create it with color!

❶ Draw a simple design that is easy to
divide into three sections.

❷ In one section, paint dots of red close together. In the second section, paint dots of yellow, and in the third, dots of blue.

❸ Paint dots of blue next to the red, dots of red next to the yellow, and dots of yellow next to the blue.

❹ Relax your eyes to let them mix the colors together. Do you see the secondary colors where the two primaries blend?

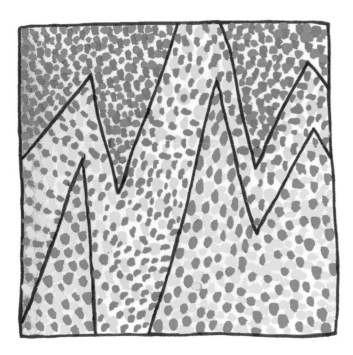

Pictures and Pixels

Printers use this idea of mixing dots of color to create the color pictures and photographs you see in magazines, books, and newspapers. In fact, these tiny dots, called *pixels*, are mixed together in differing proportions to make all the colors seen on the pages of this book. Use a magnifying glass to check it out!

The Color Wheel

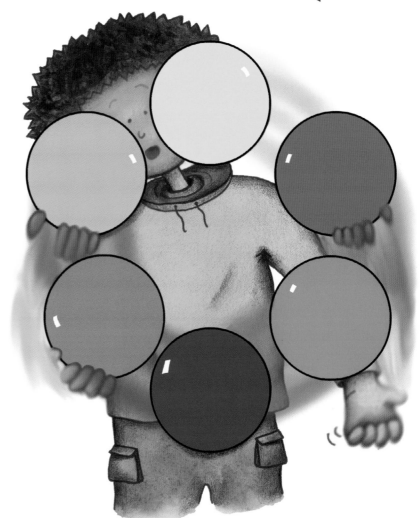

Have you noticed the shape we're creating when we show the primary (page 8) and secondary (page 20) colors arranged in that circular way? You might already know what it's called. If you said the **color wheel**, you're absolutely right! It's the perfect name for that round design of colors.

The color wheel is a really handy tool that will help you choose and combine colors for your artwork. All the colors of the color spectrum (page 10), except for indigo, are on the color wheel. Placing the colors in a circle like this shows you at a glance how they are related to each other.

The color wheel is usually shown like this, with black lines connecting the primary colors and the secondary colors.

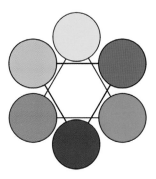

See how each secondary color is *between* the two primaries that are mixed to create it? See how the colors next to each other are more similar and the colors farther apart are more different? Red, orange, and yellow are side by side, for example. But these colors are very different from blue, green, or violet, which are on the opposite side of the wheel. The color wheel can also be shown as a pie shape (page 44).

We'll be adding to the basic color wheel later on. But let's have some fun with it first!

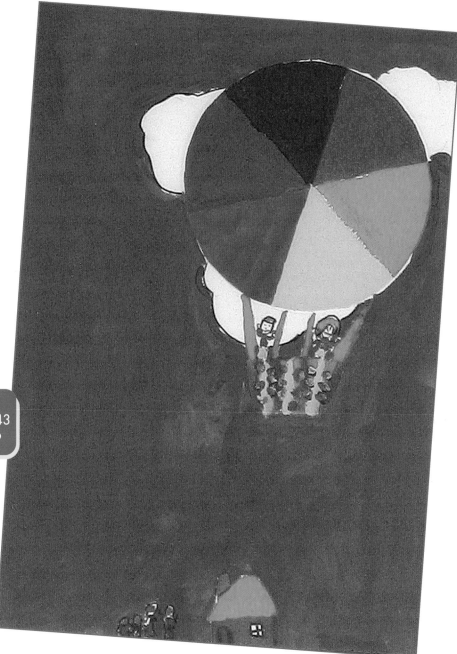

Color Wheel Creation, page 43
Meghan, age 9

Tropical Fish Fun

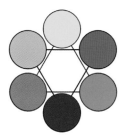

An underwater scene with brightly colored fish is a fun way to play with the colors on the color wheel. Paint a pale blue ocean background, then use all the colors to create fish of different shapes and sizes. Which colors make the fish really pop off the page?

Emily, age 9

What you need

Old newspaper to protect your work surface

Pencil

Scrap paper

Watercolor paper (9" x 12"/22.5 x 30 cm)

Masking fluid*

Watercolor paints

Paintbrush

Shallow containers for mixing paints

Container of water and paper towel to clean paintbrush between colors

Create it with color!

❶ Look at pictures of tropical fish online or in a book, or observe some real fish at a pet store or local aquarium. What are some of the typical colors? Practice drawing a few different fish shapes on scrap paper.

*nontoxic but please use in a well-ventilated room with adult help

❷ Lightly draw several fish on the watercolor paper. Vary the sizes and shapes.

❸ Paint the area inside the pencil line of each fish with the masking fluid. Let dry.

masking fluid

Gather a group of friends and paint a mural full of tropical fish! Ask permission to decorate one of the walls at your school or community center with a colorful deep-sea scene.

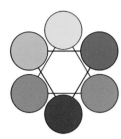

4 Paint a blue and green watercolor wash (page 39) over the entire paper. Let dry. Peel off the masking fluid.

5 Paint your fish with the primary and secondary colors.

6 Paint some seaweed and coral "growing" from the ocean floor.

A Watercolor Wash

Washes (watered-down watercolor paint brushed over the paper) create beautiful backgrounds that can then be painted over. Use a wash to represent sky, water, a sunset, or just a pale background of delicate colors.

To create a wash, put about ¹/₂" (1 cm) of water in a small container. Dab a wet paintbrush on one of the watercolor cakes and then mix it with the water in the container. Do this several times to get plenty of paint mixed in with the water. The more paint, the darker the color. Mix a separate container for each color. Tape the corners of your paper to your work surface. You can use a paintbrush or a sponge to paint the wash.

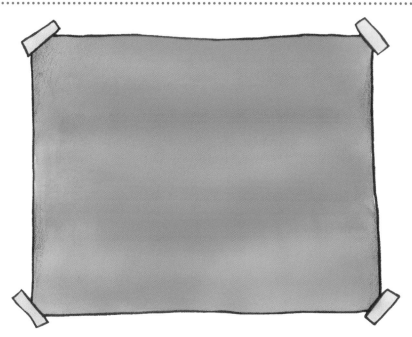

Cover your paper with wide brushstrokes of watercolor wash. Use one or more colors.

Or, with a clean sponge, wet your paper all over. Dab short strokes of watercolor wash all over the paper. Repeat with a second color.

Beautiful Bouquet

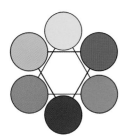

Why do you think so many artists through the years have painted bouquets of flowers? It's a simple subject, but it lets you use lots of different colors. Let the flowers be the main focus of your painting, using the bright primary and secondary colors to bring them to life.

What you need

Old newspaper to protect your work surface

Pencil

Good-quality white paper (12" x 18"/30 x 45 cm)

Scrap paper

Tempera paints in red, orange, yellow, green, blue, and violet

Paintbrushes in different sizes

Container of water and paper towel to clean paintbrushes between colors

Tom, age 10

Create it with color!

❶ Draw a horizontal line across the bottom fourth of your white paper to represent the surface of a table. Lightly draw a flower vase *below* the line so it looks as if it "sits" on the table. Make the vase big enough to hold a big bouquet of flowers.

❸ Choose a color of paint and paint one of your flower designs several times on the top two thirds of your paper.

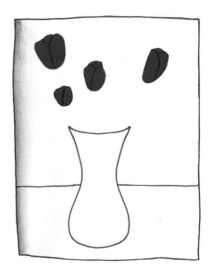

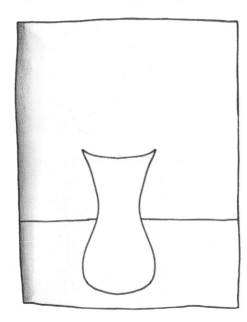

❷ For inspiration, look at pictures of flowers in a gardening catalog or book, or look at flowers outdoors. Notice the varieties of colors as well as the different sizes and shapes of the flowers. On the scrap paper, sketch five different flower shapes.

❹ Choose another color and make another flower design, repeating it several times. Continue repeating flower designs, using a different color paint for each flower.

❺ Paint green stems from the flowers to the vase. (It's not necessary to paint a stem for each flower.) Add leaves to your stems.

❻ Paint your vase and table in two colors that will show up well next to each other.

A Still-Life Painting

The bouquet of flowers you painted is an example of a *still life*. This type of painting shows objects that aren't alive — in other words, they stay still while you paint them. Can you find another piece of art in this chapter that is an example of a still life?

"I selected the blue vase for its size and shape, and for the way the strong blue color repeated some of the blues of the flowers. If you look closely at the white fabric in the background, you'll see I painted the paler colors of the bouquet in its folds. I planned the directions of the folds so they would lead the viewer's eye upward and into the bouquet."
— JANET WALSH

Cobalt Blue Vase, 1992
Janet Walsh

Color Wheel Creation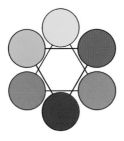

The color wheel can also look like a pie with colorful wedges (page 44). Make a pie-shaped color wheel and cut it out. Then use your imagination — and all the color-wheel colors — to turn the wheel into a picture!

Isaac, age 9

A Colorful Pie

Here are the six colors on the color wheel shown in a pie shape. The color relationship is the same — and now it really looks like a wheel!

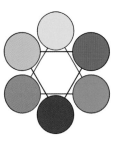

What you need

Old newspaper to protect your work surface

Good-quality white paper, 2

Pencil

Compass

Protractor

Scissors

Glue

Tempera paints in red, orange, yellow, green, blue, and violet

Paintbrush

Container of water and paper towel to clean paintbrush between colors

Create it with color!

❶ On one piece of paper, draw the color wheel as shown.

With the compass, draw a circle.

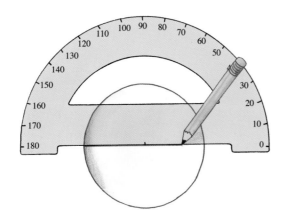

Place the straight edge of the protractor so that it goes through the center of the circle and draw a straight line that divides the circle in half.

Place the protractor on the center line. Make two marks on the top of the circle as shown.

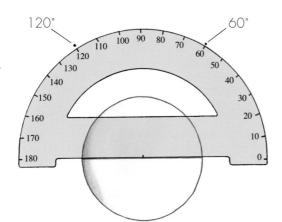

Draw a line from the 60° mark to the opposite side of the circle as shown. Repeat the process, starting at the 120° mark. This will divide your circle into six pie-shaped wedges.

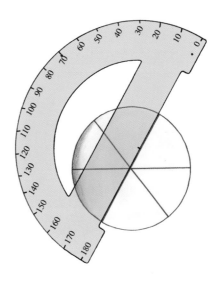

❷ Following the color wheel, paint the primary and secondary colors in the appropriate areas. Let dry. Cut out the wheel.

❸ Brainstorm ideas of how you could incorporate your color wheel into a picture. Lightly sketch out your idea on the other piece of paper. Glue the color wheel in the appropriate place. Paint your picture using the primary and secondary colors.

Fresh Fruit Delight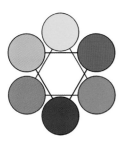

Red apples, yellow bananas, green grapes, and more! Paint a tempting bowl of fresh fruit using all six colors from the color wheel. Pile your bowl high with fruit, and fill your paper with bright bold color.

Jordan, age 9

What you need

Old newspaper to protect your work surface

Pencil

Good-quality white paper (12" x 18"/30 x 45 cm)

Fresh fruit arranged in a bowl

Tempera paints in red, orange, yellow, green, blue, and violet

Paintbrush

Container of water and paper towel to clean paintbrush between colors

Create it with color!

❶ Draw a horizontal line across the bottom third of your paper to represent the surface of a table. Draw the outline of a fruit bowl *below* the line so that bowl looks as if it is sitting on the table.

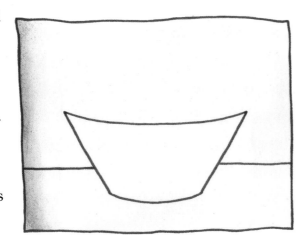

❷ Look at the real fruit, and draw fruit shapes along the edge of the bowl, showing only the parts that appear above the rim of the bowl. Make the fruit fairly big and let each piece of fruit touch the next one. Draw a few more pieces of fruit piled on top of the others to make a heaping mound of fruit.

❸ Paint your bowl, and each piece of fruit. Use all six primary and secondary colors at least once in your painting.

❹ After the initial colors are dry, paint decorative designs on your fruit bowl if you wish. This process is called *overpainting*.

The End of the Rainbow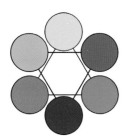

Rainbows seem almost magical when they appear in the sky. What if one landed right in your yard? Use the color-wheel colors to show what you think might happen where the colors touch the ground.

What you need

Old newspaper to protect your work surface

Pencil

Scrap paper

Watercolor paper (12" x 18"/30 x 45 cm)

Watercolor paints

Paintbrush (flat ended)

Container of water and paper towel to clean paintbrush between colors

Masking fluid*

*nontoxic but please use in a well-ventilated room with adult help

Danielle, age 9

"The rainbow ended in a pond and turned the rocks to gold." —DANIELLE

Create it with color!

❶ Take time to plan your picture, sketching it first on scrap paper if you want. Think about how you want to show the rainbow. Will you show the whole arc or just a portion of it? How will you show the ground area where it lands?

❷ Make a horizon line across the bottom fourth of your watercolor paper. Using plenty of water and paint to make a continuous stroke, paint the red arc of the rainbow. If your paint runs out before you complete the line, load your brush up again with more water and paint and go over the line, beginning at the point just before the paint ran out.

Make the next color line (orange) next to the first, following the same curved shape.

❸ Complete your rainbow with additional stripes of color. It's fine if you don't want to use all six colors of the color wheel.

❹ Once the rainbow is completely dry (you can speed up the process with a hair dryer), paint over it with masking fluid. Let dry.

❺ Paint the sky with a watercolor wash (page 39). While the paint is still wet, use a crumpled paper towel to dab off areas of paint, creating cloud shapes where the white paper shows through. Paint the ground area.

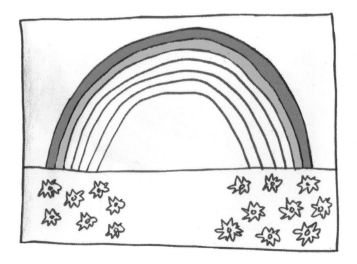

Surprise Colors

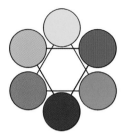

A green sky? Orange and blue horses? This painting uses the primary and secondary colors in a playful way to catch your attention. So go a little color crazy! Paint a picture of ordinary objects using unusual colors in a way that will surprise the viewer.

Jordan, age 9

What you need

Old newspaper to protect your work surface

Watercolor paper

Pencil

Watercolor paints

Paintbrush

Container of water and paper towel to clean paintbrush between colors

Create it with color!

① Draw a simple picture that has recognizable objects such as a landscape, an animal, or a portrait.

② Think about the colors you would use to make your painting look realistic, such as green grass and blue sky. Then think about how to paint those same objects with unusual and unexpected colors.

Using Color in Art Then

The German painter **Franz Marc** was an artist who knew how to use his imagination. His favorite subjects were animals in nature. Marc often used really unusual colors to paint ordinary things, and his color choices had symbolic meaning. He would use yellow, for example, to show gentleness or cheerfulness. Visit the Solomon R. Guggenheim Museum's website (RESOURCES, page 125) to view the painting *Yellow Cow*, which Franz painted in 1911. Do you think his use of yellow goes well with the cow's expression?

Warm & Cool Colors

Some colors definitely create the feeling of warmth, while others have a cool feeling. These color families are known as *warm colors* and *cool colors*. Each family includes both primary (page 8) and secondary (page 20) colors. And you know what? The handy color wheel (pages 34 to 35) shows us that relationship, too.

The **warm colors** remind us of things like fire and heat. See how they almost jump forward?

On the other hand, the **cool colors** seem to move back. It's not that they aren't as colorful. They just remind us of other things, so they have a different effect and you can use them to create a different mood.

For example, think about the cool, refreshing qualities of water. Maybe you picture a deep, *blue* ocean or the inviting *blue* water of a swimming pool. In certain light, even ice and snow can have a *blue* tint. And when you're feeling cold, what color are your lips?

Now think about when you get hot or embarrassed. Your face turns a bright shade of *red*. Think of a sunrise or a sunset. The sky turns shades of *red* and *orange*. How about the colors you see when you look at the dancing flames of firelight? It's those same warm colors of *red*, *orange*, and *yellow*.

When you color your art, use the cool colors for images that you want to have fade into the background. Use warm colors for those you want to have pop right off the page.

African Sunset
Tyler, age 12

Can't you just feel the heat from this warm-color desert scene almost radiating off the page? Compare this painting with the cool-color snow people on pages 56 and 57.

Windblown Leaves

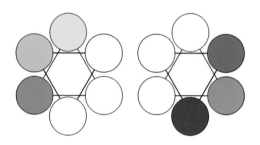

If you live in a part of the country where the leaves turn brilliant colors in the fall, you know how those oranges, reds, and yellows almost glow, especially on a sunny day. How could you make those warm, bright colors have the same effect in a painting? Try them on a cool-color background and just see what happens!

Notice how the warm colors of the leaves seem to "pop" right out of Jenna's painting.

Jenna, age 7

What you need

Old newspaper to protect your work surface

Watercolor paints

Shallow containers for mixing watercolors, 3

Paintbrush

Good-quality watercolor paper (9" x 12"/22.5 x 30 cm)

Tempera paints in red, orange, and yellow

Paper plates for mixing tempera paints

Leaves of different shapes and sizes

Container of water and paper towel to clean paintbrush between colors

Create it with color!

① Use green, blue, and violet watercolors to paint a wash (page 39) over your paper to make a "cool" sky. Let dry.

② Pour small puddles of red, orange, and yellow tempera paints onto the paper plates. Paint the front side of a leaf with a combination of these "warm colors."

③ Gently lay the leaf (paint side down) on your paper. Press gently. Peel off the leaf and discard. Repeat with additional leaves.

Laura, age 8

What happens when you reverse the color relationship? Trace around a few leaves onto watercolor paper. This time, paint the leaves with cool colors and the background with warm colors. See what you did just by switching the colors? That's how easy it is to use color in interesting ways in your art!

A Very Cool Snow Person

When you're going to paint a snowy scene, what color do you reach for first? White, of course, because it's the color of snow. How could you make your white paint feel even "cooler" in your painting? Mixing in the cool colors will create soft, cool *tints* (page 78) of those colors. Try using them to paint a snow person that will make you shiver!

What you need

Old newspaper to protect your work surface

Paper plates for mixing paints

Tempera paints in green, blue, violet, and white

Sponge brush (small piece of a clean sponge)

Blue or white construction paper
(12" x 18"/30 x 45 cm)

Paintbrush

Container of water and paper towel to clean paintbrush between colors

Kaitlin, age 8

Create it with color!

❶ On a paper plate, mix a small amount of a cool color into a puddle of white paint. Use your sponge brush to dab on this tint in a large circle shape near the bottom of your paper (leave a bit of the paper showing through between dabs of paint).

❷ On another plate, mix another cool color into some white paint and sponge-paint a medium circle above the first circle.

❸ Mix the remaining cool color with white and create a smaller circle shape for a head.

blue mixed with white

green mixed with white

violet mixed with white

❹ Use your cool tints to sponge-paint "snow" on the ground and in the air.

❺ Use the paintbrush and the cool colors green, blue, and violet to add details such as a hat, scarf, arms, and a face.

Matthew, age 8

Tree in Two Seasons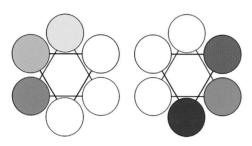

Zia, age 12

Pale, delicate watercolor paints are an excellent choice for painting a soft background sky that will show off the subject of your painting without overshadowing it. Using cool colors like blue or violet for the sky give the feel of a cold winter day. What kind of day or what season will a warm-color sky remind you of?

Brrr! The cool background colors add to the wintry feeling created by the snow and the bare tree branches.

Even though the green grass and leaves create a feeling of cool shade, what effect does the background have on the overall painting?

What you need

Old newspaper to protect your work surface

Good-quality white paper
(9" x 12"/22.5 x 30 cm)

Pencil

Graphite paper (similar to carbon paper;
available at art supply stores)

Watercolor paper (9" x 12"/22.5 x 30 cm), 2

Brown or black crayon

Watercolor paints

Shallow containers for mixing paints, 3

Paintbrushes

Tempera paints in white, green, yellow, and red

Container of water and paper towel to clean
paintbrushes between colors

Create it with color!

❶ On the white paper, draw a large tree that fills
up your paper. (Look at a real tree or a picture
of a tree if you need to.)

❷ Place the graphite paper on top of a sheet of
watercolor paper and place the tree drawing on
top of that. Trace over the outline of your tree.

graphite paper   watercolor paper

Repeat on the other sheet of watercolor paper
so you have two matching trees.

3 Pressing hard with a crayon, color in both tree shapes. Draw a horizon line across your paper near the bottom edge (but not over the tree) so that the tree looks "planted" in the ground.

4 On one tree, paint a watercolor wash (page 39) using green, blue, and violet watercolor paints to create a "winter" sky. Paint right over the tree — the crayon will resist the paint. Let dry.

5 On the other paper, paint a wash with the warm watercolors red, orange, and yellow to create a "summer" sky. Let dry.

6 On the picture with the cool sky, use white tempera paint to add snow to the crooks of the branches and along one side of the tree and branches. Paint snow on the ground.

7 On the warm-sky picture, dab green tempera paint on the branches of the trees for leaves and on the ground for grass. Try making some different greens. Mixing a little bit of yellow with the green paint will make a bright yellow green, for example. What would happen to the green if you added a bit of red to it? Use these new colors of green to add interest.

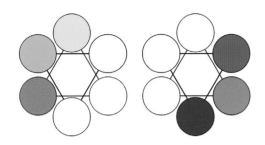

More Colorful Ideas!

Use these warm-color and cool-color methods to make spring and fall tree pictures. Then hang the pictures in a group to show the changing seasons. Can you see how the mood of the picture changes depending on the background color?

"When I begin a painting, I think in terms of temperature, and I choose mostly warm colors or cool colors to set the mood. The warm reds and yellows in this painting create the feeling of a summer day. Often I'll add a warm color to a cool area to change it. For example, I added some yellow to the green in the tree area. See how it changes the mood as well as the color? And I always add a bit of pure cool color in a warm painting — the man's blue shirt, for example — to draw attention to the surrounding warm colors."

—JOE MILLER

Untitled, 2004
Joe Miller

Warm & Cool Design

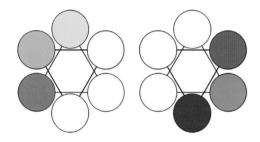

You can see from their position on the color wheel that warm colors and cool colors are opposite from each other. Well, this symmetrical design will show you that as well but in a much more artistic way!

Brian, age 8

What you need

Old newspaper to protect your work surface

Ruler

Pencil

Watercolor paper

Watercolor paints

Paintbrush

Container of water and paper towel to clean paintbrush between colors

Create it with color!

1 Use the ruler to draw two lines as shown, forming a big X on your paper.

2 Paint a symmetrical, or mirror-image, design using warm colors in two triangles opposite one another.

3 In the remaining two triangles, paint a symmetrical design using cool colors.

 Symmetry

A *symmetrical design* is one where the images on both sides of a center line match. One side is the mirror image of the other. For another symmetrical design, see pages 64 and 65.

Beautiful Butterflies

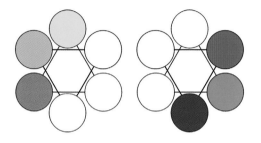

Let the butterfly, one of the most colorful insects, inspire your artwork! Make two beautiful butterflies, using warm colors to paint one insect and cool colors to paint the other.

Brent Levi, age 7

What group of colors did Brent Levi use to paint this butterfly?

What you need

Old newspaper to protect your work surface

Good-quality white paper (9" x 12"/22.5 x 30 cm), 2

Pencil

Scissors

Tempera paints in red, orange, yellow, green, blue, and violet

Paintbrush

Container of water and paper towel to clean paintbrush between colors

Create it with color!

❶ Look at a field guide or visit a nature web site to look at colorful pictures of butterflies.

❷ Fold the paper in half. Using the fold as the center line, draw half of a butterfly shape. Cut it out. Open flat.

fold

Make the upper wing larger than the lower wing.

❸ Choose a cool color of paint and paint dots on one half of your butterfly shape.

While the paint is still wet, fold the paper in half and press. Unfold.

Open to reveal matching designs on both wings.

❹ Repeat step 3 with additional cool colors of paint to make spots and lines.

❺ Paint a dark body on the center fold of your butterfly. Let dry.

❻ On the other piece of paper, repeat steps 2 through 5 with the warm colors of paint.

Complementary Colors

Complementary colors — sounds as if they would get along really well, doesn't it? But complementary colors are opposites! They aren't new colors, actually. You already know about them. The term **complementary colors** describes a relationship between two colors, one primary (page 8) and one secondary (page 20). These two colors are as different from each other as they can be. Orange and blue are complementary colors, for example. See how they sit directly opposite each other on the color wheel?

yellow
(complement of violet)

orange
(complement of blue)

green
(complement of red)

red
(complement of green)

blue
(complement of orange)

violet
(complement of yellow)

Why, Violet, you're looking vivacious today!

Green, you're just gorgeous!

My, Orange, you look outrageous!

There's a simple explanation behind this color relationship, so let's take a closer look. As you know, each secondary color is created by mixing two primaries. And here's the key: The third, *missing* primary color is that secondary color's complement.

Orange, for example, is the complement of blue, because orange contains the two primaries red and yellow, but *not* the third one, blue.

The colors in each of these pairs *complement* (show off or enhance) each other just because they're so different, so you can use them side by side in your art for a strong impact. You can also mix two complementary colors in equal amounts to form a richer-looking gray than the gray you create when you mix black and white (page 113).

 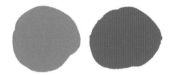 

Complementary Color Pairs

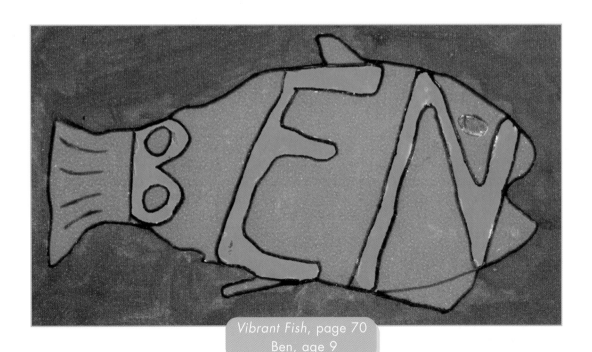

Vibrant Fish, page 70
Ben, age 9

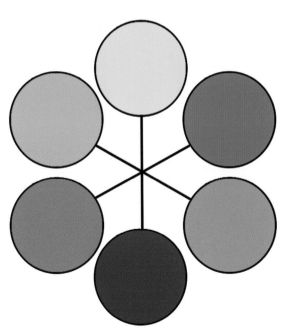

Complementary Color Wheel

Complementary-Color Blend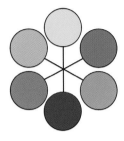

When a color is mixed with a little bit of its complementary color, it lowers the *intensity* of the original color and makes it appear dull. This painting uses the complementary colors of red and green. Watch what happens as you mix those colors in different proportions. Try several shapes, painted with different pairs of complementary colors.

Laura, age 10

Notice how the gray in the center, created by mixing a pair of complementary colors, has a bit of color to it.

What you need

Old newspaper to protect your work surface

Pencil

Scrap paper

Good-quality white paper (9" x 12"/22.5 x 30 cm)

Tape

Tempera paints in red and green

Paintbrush

Container of water and paper towel
to clean paintbrush between colors

Paper plates for mixing paints

Create it with color!

❶ Try inventing some
interesting new
shapes. Practice
drawing shapes on
scrap paper until you
get one you really like.

❷ On the white paper,
draw your shape
quite large so that
it fills your paper.

❸ Turn the paper
over and tape
down the
edges. Paint
approximately
one fifth of
the paper with
red paint. On the
opposite side of
the paper, paint
approximately one
fifth of the area
with green paint.

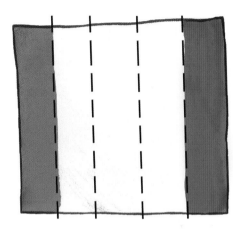

Picture your paper with four lines across it,
dividing it into five equal sections.
Each of those sections is one fifth.

❹ Mix a small
amount of green
paint with the red
and paint a stripe
of this mixture
next to your
red section. Mix
a small amount
of red paint with
green and paint
a stripe of this
mixture next to
the green paint.

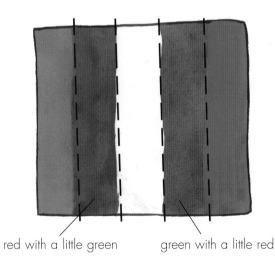

red with a little green   green with a little red

❺ Mix red and green together in equal amounts to
create a gray color and paint the center. Let dry.
Turn your paper over and cut out your shape.

Vibrant Fish

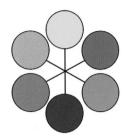

Using a pair of complementary colors, paint a fish shape, then paint your name on it. See how the letters jump out of the picture? Add a soft gray background made by mixing the two complementary colors. For more on mixing complementary colors, see COMPLEMENTARY-COLOR BLEND, pages 68 to 69.

For more on mixing complementary colors, see COMPLEMENTARY-COLOR BLEND, pages 68 to 69.

What you need

Old newspaper to protect your work surface

Pencil

Good-quality white paper (6" x 12"/15 x 30 cm)

Tempera paints in two complementary colors

Paintbrush

Container of water and paper towel to clean paintbrush between colors

Paper plate for mixing paint

Black marker

Trey, age 10

Create it with color!

❶ Draw a large fish shape, big enough to almost fill your paper. Inside the fish shape, draw bubble letters to spell your name or your initials.

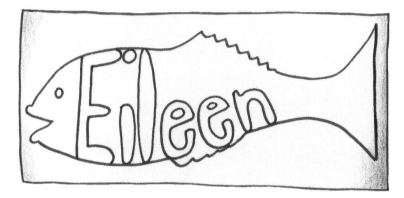

❷ Paint the letters with one of your complementary colors.

❸ Paint the surrounding area of the fish with the other complementary color.

❹ Mix the complementary colors together to make gray. Paint the background with this mixture. Let dry.

❺ Use the black marker to outline the fish and the letters to make them stand out.

Through the Artist's Eyes
Using Art in Color Today

"This painting was a birthday gift to my sister (who just happens to be the author of this book!), in honor of her beautiful flower gardens. I chose to paint an orange lily against a blue sky because, as complementary colors, they work so well together."
— PAMELA TORRES

The Happy Lily, 2001
Pamela Torres

Dancing Stripes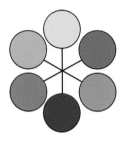

See what happens when you paint stripes of complementary colors next to each other! They contrast so strongly that they really attract attention, creating a sense of movement and energy. Black and white (page 113) aren't really complementary colors because they aren't on the color wheel, but side by side, they have the same effect.

These stripes in pairs of complementary colors seem to almost dance before your eyes!

Candice, age 11

What you need

Old newspaper to protect your work surface

Ruler

Pencil

Good-quality white paper
(12" x 18"/30 x 45 cm)

Tempera paints in red, orange, yellow,
green, blue, violet, black, and white

Paintbrush

Container of water and paper towel to
clean paintbrush between colors

Paper plate for mixing paints

Create it with color!

❶ Use the width
of the ruler to
draw a border
around the edge
of your paper.

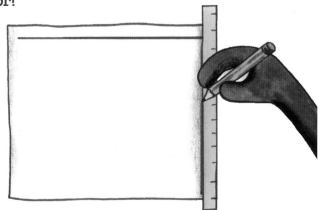

❷ Divide your paper
into four sections.
It will make the
painting more
interesting if the
lines don't go all
the way across
the paper and if
they tilt in different
directions.

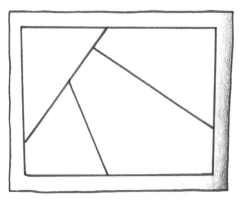

❸ Fill each section
with parallel
straight lines.

4 Decide which pairs of complementary colors you will use in each section. Start by painting every other stripe in each section with one of those colors.

In the fourth section, paint every other stripe white. Let dry.

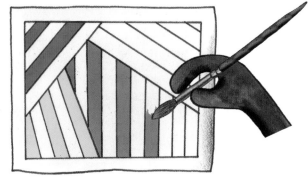

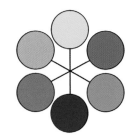

5 Paint the remaining stripes in each section with that color's complement. To complement the white, use black.

6 Mix equal amounts of each complementary-color pair together to make three slightly different grays. Paint three of the borders. Mix equal amounts of black and white together and paint the fourth border.

Cool Color Trick

Place a square of red paper on a larger piece of white paper. Stare at the red square for one minute. Remove the red square and look at the white paper and you will see an after-image of green, the complement of red.

"In this painting, I used the primary and secondary colors to explore what happens when shapes overlap each other to form fragments of the originals. To create contrast, I painted the two central circles in the complementary colors of the shapes next to them." — JESSIKA HENRY

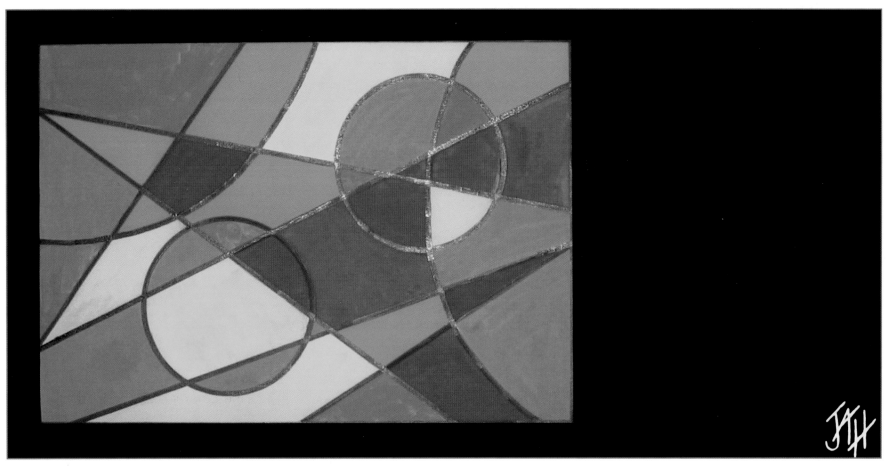

Fragmentation, 2004
Jessika Henry

Squiggle Abstract

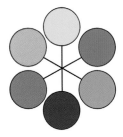

When two complementary colors are placed next to each other in a painting, they really pop out at you because they contrast so strongly. See how striking the effect of these two complementary colors is? The colors almost seem to vibrate!

Willow, age 12

What you need

Old newspaper to protect your work surface

Watercolor paper (9" x 12"/22.5 x 30 cm)

Pencil

Ruler

Watercolor paints

Paintbrush

Container of water and paper towel to clean paintbrush between colors

Create it with color!

❶ Starting at the top left-hand corner of your paper, draw a squiggly line that goes back and forth across your paper a few times. Use the ruler to divide your paper with two or more vertical lines.

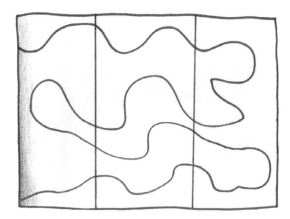

❷ Choose two complementary colors. Look at the shapes created by the squiggly line and the vertical lines. Paint all the shapes that aren't touching with one of your chosen complementary colors.

❸ Paint the remaining shapes with the other complementary color.

Color Values

Sometimes you don't need a whole new color, you just need a lighter or darker version of a particular color. When we talk about the lightness or darkness of a color, we're talking about its *value*.

When you make **light values** of a color, you're creating *tints*. To make a tint, you start with white paint, add a little bit of color, and mix together. Each time you add a little more of that same color, you create a different tint.

Tints of Blue

What do you think you would add to make **dark values** of a color, called *shades*?

If you guessed that black was added to darken this blue, you're absolutely right! When making a shade of a color, add tiny amounts of black at a time, as the black will cause the color to go dark very quickly.

Shades of Blue

When you add *both* black and white to a color, it creates a *tone*. A small amount of black and white is often added to a color to "tone it down" or make it less bright.

See how adding black and white to the color on the left tones it down?

How will you use tints, shades, and tones in your artwork? Think about how many different blues there are, from pale blue to navy blue. Think about the skin of an orange compared with a bowl of orange sherbet. You can see just how useful knowing how to paint subtle variations in color will be!

Monochromatic Design, page 81
Mariah, age 9

Creating Values with Watercolor Paints

You'll notice there's no white paint in your watercolor paints, so to create light values, or tints, of a watercolor, you use water. The more water you mix with the paint, the lighter the color value.

Let's experiment.

❶ Put a few drops of water on the red watercolor cake in your paint box. Dip your brush in water and then move it around on the red paint cake, loading the brush with red paint. Use this full-strength color to create a puddle on a mixing plate. Paint a sample of that red on watercolor paper.

❷ Add a brushful of water to the red puddle. Paint a sample on your paper. Notice that the new color is lighter in value. This is a tint of the original red.

red   tint of that red

❸ Continue to make lighter values and paint samples of each new tint.

❹ Now try going the other way. Use enough water to make a fairly light value of blue, and paint a sample on the paper. Then add more and more paint to make darker values. Try adding a little black to make even darker values, or shades.

Monochromatic Design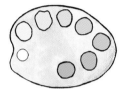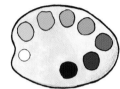

Have fun with your absolute favorite color! When something is *monochromatic* (mon-oh-kro-MAH-tick), it's created using one color or very similar colors. In a monochromatic painting, for example, you use only different values (page 78) of one particular color. Explore mixing tints (light values) and shades (dark values) in this one-color design. For another monochromatic design, see pages 117 to 118.

Derek, age 9

What you need

Old newspaper to protect your work surface

Paintbrush

Tempera paints in black, a primary or secondary color of your choice, and white

Good-quality white paper

Container of water and paper towel to clean paintbrush between colors

Paper plates for mixing paints

Create it with color!

1 Paint a black line that divides your paper in half. (The line can be curvy or jagged.) Divide each half with a line. Divide each section with a line. You now have eight areas on your paper separated by black lines. Let dry.

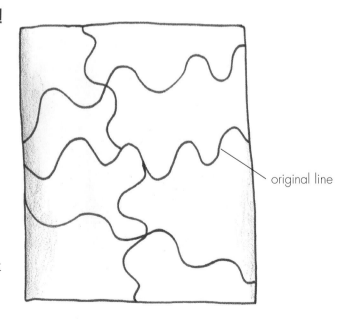

original line

2 Paint one area of your picture with the primary or secondary color.

3 Now you'll paint three other sections with tints of that color:

On a paper plate, mix a small amount of the color into a puddle of white paint. Paint one area with this lighter tint.

Mix a little more color into that light tint to make a darker tint. Paint another area.

Add more color to make an even darker tint. Paint a third area with this mixture.

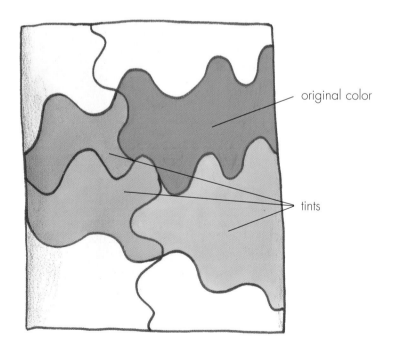

original color

tints

❹ Now paint three areas with shades of your color:

Add a very small amount of black to a puddle of your original color. Paint a section. Make two darker shades, adding a tiny amount of black each time, and paint two areas with these mixtures.

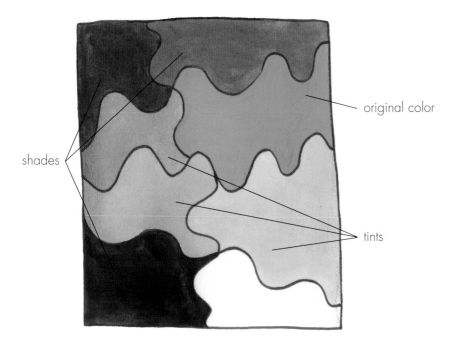

original color

shades

tints

❺ Make a tone (page 79) by mixing your original color with small amounts of black and white. Paint the final area with this mixture.

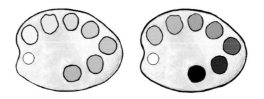

Meet the Masters!

Using Color in Art Then

Sometimes artists use a monochromatic color scheme in their paintings to create a mood or express a feeling. What color do you associate with sadness? A lot of people think of blue, and there's even an expression "to feel blue," which means to feel sad.

Pablo Picasso was a Spanish painter and sculptor who died in 1973. During an extremely difficult period in his life, Picasso painted several monochromatic paintings in blue. Take a look at *The Tragedy* at the web site of the National Gallery of Art in Washington, D.C. (RESOURCES, page 125). How do the people look? How has Picasso created that feeling?

Blossom Time

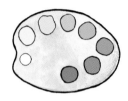

Experiment with adding small amounts of red paint to white to create different tints (page 78) for the petals on this tree. A sponge brush is perfect for making tiny dots of paint to suggest delicate petals.

What you need

Old newspaper to protect your work surface

Paper towel

Light blue construction paper (12" x 18"/30 x 45 cm)

Pencil

Ruler

Crayons

Tempera paints in white and red

Paper plates for mixing paints

Sponge brush (small piece of clean sponge)

Alex, age 7

Create it with color!

❶ On the blue paper, lightly sketch a tree. Look at a real tree or a picture of a tree if that's helpful, but don't worry if your tree doesn't look exactly like the one you're drawing. Position the tree on your paper as shown.

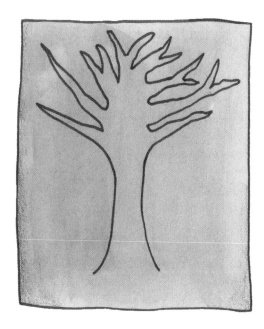

Make the base of the trunk at least 2" (5 cm) from bottom the paper.

Color the tree with a brown crayon.

❷ About 4" (10 cm) from the bottom of the paper, draw a horizontal line across your paper, going behind the tree, to represent the ground and make your tree look as if it's growing. Color in the area below the line with a green crayon.

❸ Pour three small puddles of white paint onto separate plates. Add varying amounts of red to each puddle to make three different tints of red.

Dip your sponge brush in the darkest tint and dab dots on the branches of your tree for petals. Leave a bit of paper showing between the dabs of paint.

❹ Repeat with the other tints of paint, using the lightest tint last. Dab paint on the ground area to represent fallen petals.

Moonlit Night

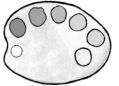 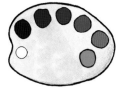

Here's a cool visual trick that uses only values (page 78) of blue! In this painting, the *focal point* (the part of the painting that your eye is drawn to right away) is the moon. Tints and shades of blue, used to paint radiating circles that get larger and darker, then draw your eye outward. The stark, black shapes of the house and tree complete this nighttime scene.

Jasa, age 12

What you need

Old newspaper to protect your work surface

Good-quality white paper

Ruler

Pencil

Tempera paints in blue, white, and black

Sponge brush (small piece of clean sponge)

Paper plates for mixing paints

Container of water and paper towel to clean sponge brush between colors

Paintbrush

Create it with color!

❶ Find the center of your paper with your finger. Move your finger up about 2" (5 cm) and over to the right about 2" (5 cm) and make a pencil mark. Use the sponge brush to paint a small circle of white on the mark to represent the moon.

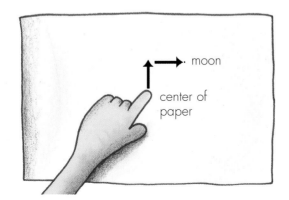

moon

center of paper

❷ Add a small amount of blue paint to a puddle of white paint and mix together. Sponge-paint a ring of this tint around the dot of white.

❸ Continue making values (tints) of blue by adding a little more blue paint to the mixture and then painting a ring of color. When you get to a place where a complete circle no longer fits on the paper, paint just the part that does fit. Fill the paper with radiating circles of blue.

❹ To completely fill the page, you may need to add even darker values of blue. To make these shades of blue, add a tiny bit of black to blue; add the black in *very* small amounts as it will quickly make your color go dark.

lighter values of blue (tints)

a darker value of blue made with black (a shade)

❺ Use black paint to make a simple silhouette scene along the bottom edge of the picture.

Meet the Masters!

Using Color in Art Then

Vasily Kandinsky (page 19), a Russian painter who painted in the early 1900s, believed that feelings and ideas could be expressed using only shapes, lines, colors, and textures, and so his style of abstract art (page 16) is called *expressionism*. Kandinsky loved music, so he made colors and shapes move across his paintings as if they were expressing or representing a melody.

Study the painting shown here. You won't see recognizable images, but do you think Kandinsky did a good job of using color to express feeling and movement? Notice the name of the painting. Kandinsky called many of his paintings "improvisations," which can mean songs made up on the spot.

Vasily Kandinsky
Improvisation 28 (second version), 1912
Oil on canvas
43 7/8 x 63 7/8 inches (111.4 x 162.1 cm)
Solomon R. Guggenheim Museum, New York
Gift, Solomon R. Guggenheim, 1937
37.239

Color Dance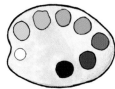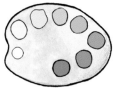

Let music inspire your creation of an abstract painting (page 16) just as Vasily Kandinsky did many years ago. As you listen to some music, draw and paint a small portion of what you hear. Create tints and shades (page 78) of different intensities. Use bold shapes and dark colors for the more dramatic parts of the music, and lighter colors and more delicate shapes for the softer parts.

Noah, age 8

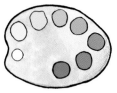

What you need

Classical music (a symphony works especially well)

Old newspaper to protect your work surface

Scrap paper

Pencil

Watercolor paper

Watercolor paints

Paintbrush

Shallow containers for mixing paints

Container of water and paper towel to clean your paintbrush between colors

Black permanent marker

Create it with color!

❶ Listen to some music and draw a variety of lines that express the feel and sound of the music. Make at least three samples and choose your favorite.

❷ Draw similar lines on the watercolor paper. Extend some of your lines so they touch the edge of the paper or one of the other lines, creating some interesting shapes.

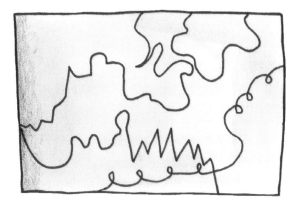

❸ Choose a color and mix light values of it (page 80). Use them to paint two or three areas of your design. Let the music lines help you determine where to paint.

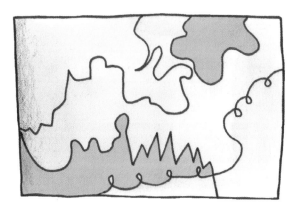

④ Repeat step 3 with one or more colors, filling your paper with light values of paint.

Repeating colors throughout the picture will create movement and balance.

⑤ Make darker values (page 80) of each color by adding more paint to the mixtures (the more paint, the darker the color). Paint these darker values along some of your music lines.

Inside some areas, experiment with gradually changing from dark to light values.

⑥ Study your painting. Add more lines and shapes in other colors, as you like. To make some of the music lines really stand out, go over them with the black marker.

3-D Bottle

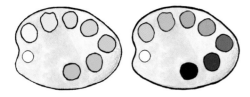

Want to make a painting of a simple object, such as a bottle, look as realistic as possible? First, make it look three-dimensional by using dark values (page 78) of a color to show the side of the bottle farthest from the light source. Then add the shadow the bottle is casting.

Laura, age 11

What you need

Old newspaper to protect your work surface

Bottle

Desk lamp or spotlight

Scrap paper

Pencil

Scissors

Watercolor paper

Watercolor paints

Paintbrush

Shallow container for mixing paints

Container of water and paper towel to clean paintbrush between colors

Create it with color!

❶ Place the bottle on a table and shine the lamp on it from the side so a shadow is formed. What are some of the things you notice about the shape of the shadow cast by the bottle? Where is the shadow darkest?

❷ On scrap paper, draw the outline of the bottle. If you want to be sure your bottle is symmetrical (exactly the same on both sides), draw half a bottle shape on a folded piece of paper and cut it out.

Cut out a half bottle shape and unfold it.

Trace the unfolded shape onto the watercolor paper. Be sure to position the bottle on the paper so that you'll have enough space to paint the shadow.

❸ Lightly draw a line behind the bottle to represent the edge of the table as shown in the finished picture on page 92. See how the bottle now looks as if it's sitting on the table?

❹ Choose a primary or secondary color of paint. Place a drop of water on that watercolor cake to soften it. Dip your brush into the paint and paint a spot of color in your container. Add a brushful of water and mix to make a lighter value. Paint your bottle shape with this color.

❺ Add more paint to the puddle in the container to create a darker value. Paint a stripe of that color in the center of the bottle.

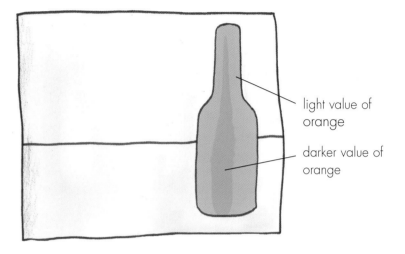

light value of orange

darker value of orange

❻ Add more paint to the puddle to make an even darker value. Paint this color on the side farthest from the light source. How does this paint make the bottle look?

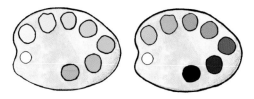

❼ Blend the different values together by painting over the bottle shape with a wet brush.

❽ Mix your original color with its complement (page 66) to make a neutral gray. Use it to paint the shadow the bottle is casting on the table. Let dry.

Paint the table with the bottle's complementary color. Let dry.

Paint the wall behind the table a different color.

"My inspiration for this painting came after a fresh snowfall on a moonlit night. The full moon shining on the snow cast very distinct and beautiful shadows. The blue tones I selected deepened the shadow areas and using softened values captured the quiet mood and the cool, wintry atmosphere."

—TERA BELK

Silent Night, 2001
Tera Belk

Intermediate & Analogous Colors

Intermediate Colors

Now you know how to use six colors — three primary and three secondary — really effectively, lightening them, darkening them, and combining them in striking ways. But what about those times you need something sort of in-between? Well, there are still a few colors to add to the color wheel. They're called the **intermediate colors**.

To create the six *intermediate colors*, you mix a primary color (page 8) with a neighboring secondary color (page 20). The name of each intermediate color is really easy to remember — it tells you what two colors were used to make it. Red-violet, for example, is made by mixing equal amounts of primary red and secondary violet.

So from what you now know about color relationships, when we add the intermediate colors to the color wheel, where would you expect to find them? That's right, they're *between* the two colors used to mix them. You can see the intermediate color wheel, showing all 12 colors, on page 98.

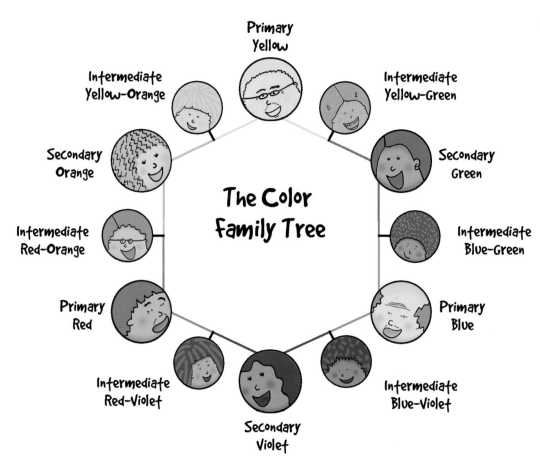

The primary and secondary colors, with their intermediate "relatives"

Mix the Six!

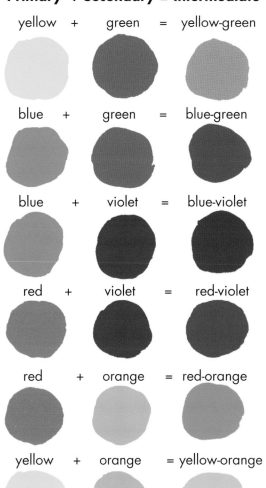

Primary + Secondary = Intermediate

yellow + green = yellow-green

blue + green = blue-green

blue + violet = blue-violet

red + violet = red-violet

red + orange = red-orange

yellow + orange = yellow-orange

This intriguing design uses light and dark values (page 78) of a range of intermediate colors.

Color Grid, page 105
Colleen, age 9

Analogous Colors

Certain colors that are side by side on the intermediate color wheel can be grouped together and referred to as **analogous colors**.

Think of these colors as a family, because they are related. The word *analogous* (an-AL-oh-gus) means things that show a likeness to each other, and you can see that, just like members of many families, these colors resemble each other.

But don't worry, you don't need to memorize groups of colors to use the analogous colors in your artwork — just refer to the handy color wheel!

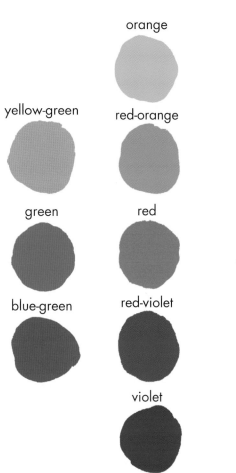

orange

yellow-green   red-orange

green   red

blue-green   red-violet

violet

Here are two analogous color families. Can you see that the colors in each family have a similar look?

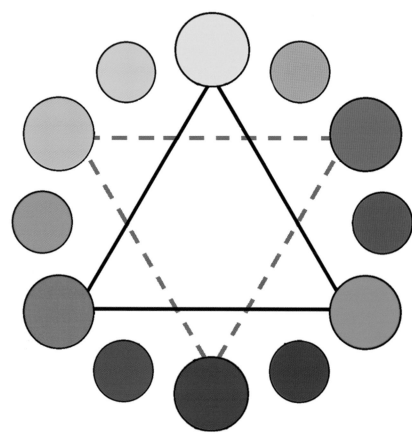

See how easy it is to find the analogous colors side by side on the intermediate color wheel?

Any analogous color can be mixed with its color-wheel neighbor without becoming dull or gray to make subtle new colors. When you use analogous colors together in a painting, it creates a feeling of harmony. In other words, these colors look nice with each other!

Pulled-Apart Puzzle
Cody, age 10

Shapes in the analogous colors of yellow-green, green, and blue-green show up well against a background painted with green's complementary color (page 66) of red.

Stained Glass Window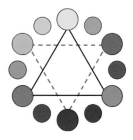

Primary and secondary colors blend together to make intermediate colors in this watercolor design. These subtle, "in-between" colors are perfect for creating the look of a stained glass window.

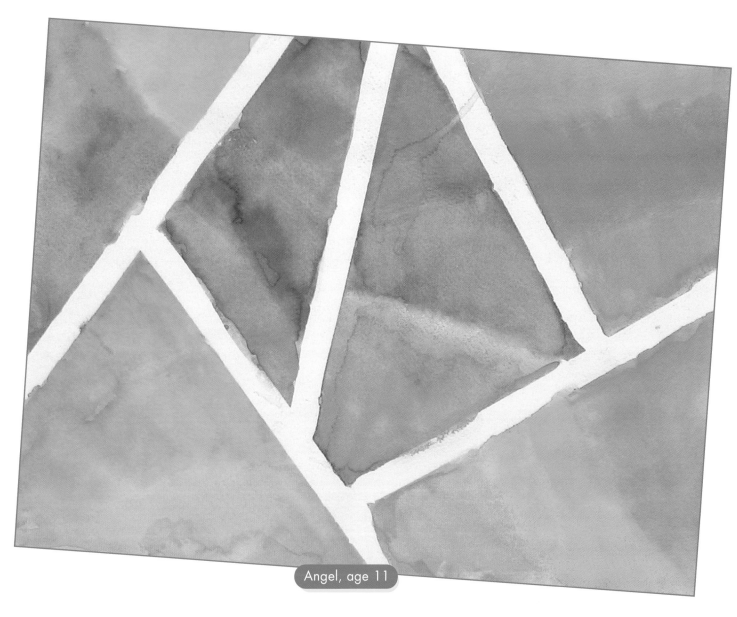

Angel, age 11

What you need

Old newspaper to protect your work surface

Masking tape

Watercolor paper (9" x 12"/22.5 x 30 cm)

Watercolor paints

Paintbrush

Container of water and paper towel to clean paintbrush between colors

Create it with color!

❶ Apply masking tape to your paper to create six angled shapes.

❷ Put a drop of water onto each watercolor cake. Dampen the paintbrush and go over one color to soften it.

❸ Paint a third of one shape in a primary color. Paint another third of that shape with a neighboring secondary color as shown.

In the lid of your paint box, mix the two colors together to create an intermediate color. Paint the middle third with this new color.

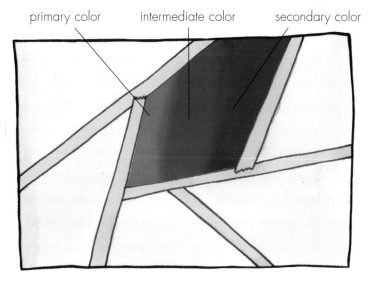

primary color   intermediate color   secondary color

❹ Repeat the process in each of the other shapes, using new combinations of primary, secondary, and intermediate colors from an analogous color family. Refer to the color wheel, if necessary. Let dry.

❺ Carefully peel off the masking tape to reveal a colorful stained glass window.

Meet the Masters!

Using Art in Color Then

Artist **Paul Klee** (pronounced "clay") was a Swiss painter born in 1879. Fascinated by color and light, Klee said, "Color and I are one." He used colors to portray a feeling or a mood in the painting style known as expressionism. (For another expressionist painter, see page 88).

　　Klee painted several similar paintings that he called the Magic Square series. These squares of color were placed in a certain way to make your eyes move around the painting.

　　Look carefully at Klee's painting. Can you pick out the intermediate colors? How does the placement of those colors make your eyes move around the painting? What if Klee hadn't used dark colors around the edges — how would the overall effect be different?

Paul Klee
New Harmony (Neue Harmonie), 1936
Oil on canvas
36⁷/8 x 26¹/8 inches (93.6 x 66.3 cm); 71.1960
Solomon R. Guggenheim Museum, New York

Magic Square Design

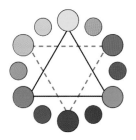

Make a magic square painting in the style of the artist Paul Klee. Explore mixing the intermediate colors, and changing them into different tints and shades (page 78). Can you use these colors to create a sense of movement in your painting? Think about where you want the viewer's eyes to go and use the colors to guide them.

Danielle, age 9

What you need

Old newspaper to protect your work surface

Pencil

Yardstick (meter stick)

Good-quality white paper

Tempera paints in red, orange, yellow, green, blue, violet, black, and white

Paper plate for mixing paint

Paintbrush

Container of water and paper towel to clean paintbrush between colors

Create it with color!

❶ Draw lines on your paper to divide it as shown.

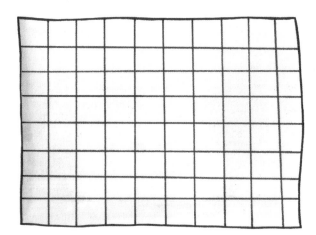

❷ Mix red and orange together to make the intermediate color red-orange. Paint some of your squares with this color.

❸ Add white to a portion of the mixture to make a lighter value (page 78) of red-orange. Paint a square or two with this tint.

Add a small amount of black to the rest of the red-orange paint to create a darker value, or shade. Paint a square with this color.

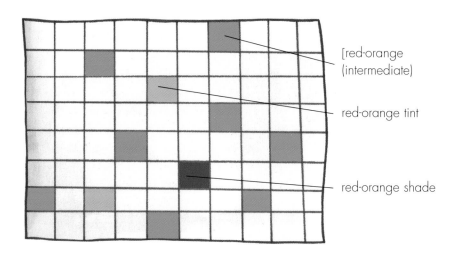

[red-orange (intermediate)

red-orange tint

red-orange shade

❹ Refering to the color wheel, mix the other intermediate colors and their tints and shades to complete your picture.

Color Grid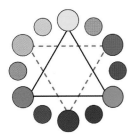

See how these shapes, painted in analogous colors (page 98), hold together as one color-related unit? Yet at the same time, they really pop out against the black and white background of squares.

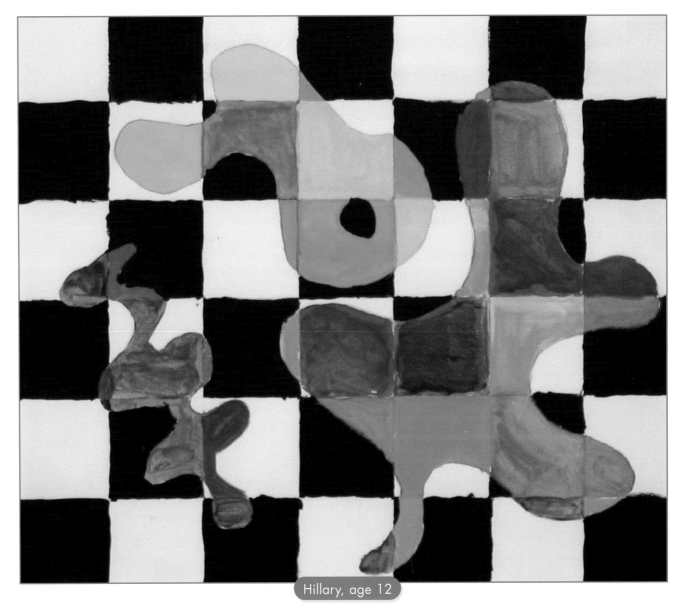

Hillary, age 12

What you need

Old newspaper to protect your work surface

Yardstick (meter stick)

Pencil

Good-quality white paper (12" x 18"/30 x 45 cm), 2

Scissors

Tempera paints in red, orange, yellow, green, blue, violet, black, and white

Paintbrush

Paper plates for mixing paints

Container of water and paper towel to clean paintbrush between colors

Create it with color!

❶ Measure and mark around the edges of one sheet of paper as shown. Connect the marks with horizontal and vertical lines to create a grid.

2" (5 cm)

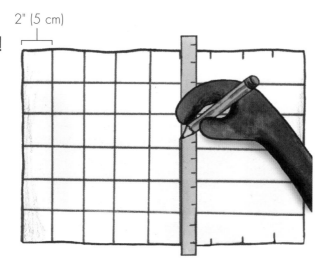

❷ On the other piece of paper, draw five interesting-looking shapes. Cut them out. Position all or some of the shapes on your grid paper and trace around them.

❸ Pick a family of three analogous colors (refer to the color wheel if you need to). Paint one shape with the colors, mixing paints as necessary. The lines on the grid show you where to change colors.

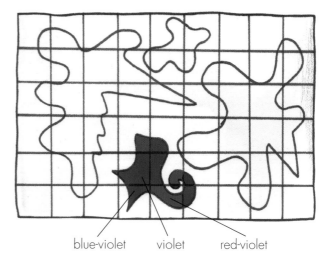

blue-violet   violet   red-violet

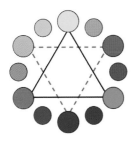

Choose a family of analogous colors. Using a small piece of a clean sponge, sponge-paint circles of those colors radiating out from the center as you move clockwise around the color wheel (page 98). Start with violet, for example, followed by red-violet, red, red-orange, and orange.

Make two more paintings with other analogous families. Group them to form a colorful abstract painting.

❹ Now paint a different shape. Try using one of the five-color families, such as the one shown here.

orange

yellow-orange

yellow

yellow-green

green

Paint the remaining shapes, using different sets of analogous colors.

❺ Paint the background in a black-and-white checkerboard pattern as shown in the finished painting on page 105.

Meet the Masters!

Using Art in Color Then

Compare how two artists with very different styles who painted at about the same time used analogous colors to paint a scene from nature. Look at *Mountains at Saint-Rémy* (1889) by the Dutch painter **Vincent Van Gogh** (van GO) on the Solomon R. Guggenheim Museum's website (RESOURCES, page 125). Then take an online look at *The Japanese Footbridge* (1899) by French painter **Claude Monet** (mo-NAY) at the National Gallery of Art in Washington, D.C. Which style do you prefer?

Overlapping Shapes

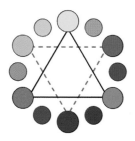

Use a repeating shape made with primary, secondary, and intermediate colors that follow their order on color wheel. Can you figure out why the painting shows 11 colors and the intermediate color wheel shows 12? Think about a design you could create to show all 12 colors.

Angel, age 11

What you need

Old newspaper to protect your work surface

Pencil

Jar lid, cookie cutter, or other small object for tracing

Cardstock or other stiff paper

Scissors

Good-quality white paper (9" x 12"/22.5 x 30 cm)

Tempera paints in red, orange, yellow, green, blue, and violet

Paintbrush

Paper plates for mixing paints

Container of water and paper towel to clean paintbrush between colors

Create it with color!

❶ Trace the object onto the cardstock and cut it out. Trace around this paper shape six times on the white paper so that each shape overlaps a portion of the previous one as shown.

❷ Paint the shapes in the primary and secondary colors. Start with any primary or secondary color and follow the order of the colors around the color wheel. Don't paint where the shapes overlap.

❸ Mix an intermediate color by combining a primary color with a neighboring secondary color. Paint the overlapping area between those two neighboring colors. Continue mixing and painting in the other overlapping areas.

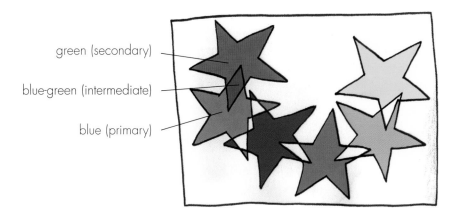

green (secondary)

blue-green (intermediate)

blue (primary)

The American painter **Georgia O'Keeffe** began painting in the early 1900s. She is well known for her very large, detailed flower portraits that were inspired by the summers she spent in the country in northern New York. She made her flower pictures extra large, so that the wonderful details could be seen, and used related colors like analogous colors to show shading and the delicate beauty of the blossom.

"Nobody sees a flower, really. It is so small. We haven't time. So I said to myself, I'll paint what I see ... but I'll paint it big and they will be surprised into taking time to look at it." — GEORGIA O'KEEFFE

Georgia O'Keeffe
White Iris, 1930
Oil on canvas
40 x 30 in. (100 x 75 cm)

Virginia Museum of Fine Arts, Richmond
Gift of Mr. and Mrs. Bruce C. Gottwald
Photo: Katherine Wetzel
© Virginia Museum of Fine Arts

Flower Power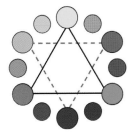

Observe the details of a flower, then paint it, making it extra large in the style of Georgia O'Keeffe. Use the closely related analogous colors to show the shape of the individual flower petals and the delicate shading in the center of the flower.

Audrey, age 11

What you need

Old newspaper to protect your work surface

Flower blossom or a picture of one

Good-quality white paper
(18" x 18"/45 x 45 cm)

Pencil

Cardstock

Scissors

Tempera paints in red, orange, yellow,
green, blue, violet, and white

Paintbrush

Container of water and paper towel to
clean paintbrush between colors

Paper plate for mixing paints

Create it with color!

❶ Look closely the flower, carefully observing the shape of the petals and the delicate details in the center. On the white paper, draw the center of your flower (it doesn't have to be in the middle of your paper).

❷ Draw a large petal shape on the cardstock and cut it out. Trace around it to make matching petals radiating out from the center of the flower. Some of the petals may not completely fit on the paper.

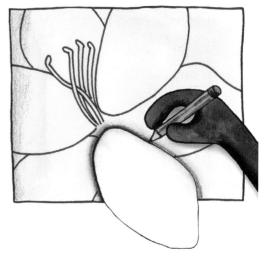

❸ Choose three or five analogous colors. (Refer to the color wheel on page 111 to choose colors, if you need to.) The colors you choose don't have to match the real flower. Mix paints as necessary to create this color family and use them to paint your flower.

This flower uses the analogous family of violet, red-violet, red, red-orange, and orange.

❹ Add a little white paint to one of your colors to create a tint (page 78) of that color. Paint the background.

Neutrals

Have you noticed that some colors are missing from the color wheel? How could you paint a nighttime sky or a winter scene without black and white for example? What will you use to paint an elephant or a mouse? How about the trunk of a tree in a landscape painting? We see black, white, gray, and brown all around us and we also see them in art all the time. So why aren't they on the color wheel?

Black and **white** aren't found in the color spectrum (page 10), so they aren't considered true colors and they aren't included on the color wheel. We refer to them as colors when we're talking about paint, crayons, or fabrics, for example, but black and white are actually called **neutrals**.

Negative Space
Jessica, age 11

Black and white look intriguing when placed next to each other because they are so very different from one another.

You can mix black and white in different proportions to create many different values (page 78) of **gray**, another neutral.

Now I can paint Sparky's portrait!

SPARKY

Brown, also a neutral, is created by mixing the three primary colors together. The amount of each color in the mix determines how dark or light the brown will be. Experiment with adding a bit of one of your brown mixtures to white or black to create different skin tones.

yellow + $1/4$ of that amount of red + $1/8$ of that amount of blue = tan

red + $1/2$ that amount of yellow + $1/4$ that amount of blue = rust

equal amounts of red and yellow + $1/2$ that amount of blue = dark brown

Wise Brown Owl
Jenna, age 9

Playful Penguins

The plump body of a penguin against a snowy background is a fun way to show the stark contrast of two neutrals, black and white, side by side.

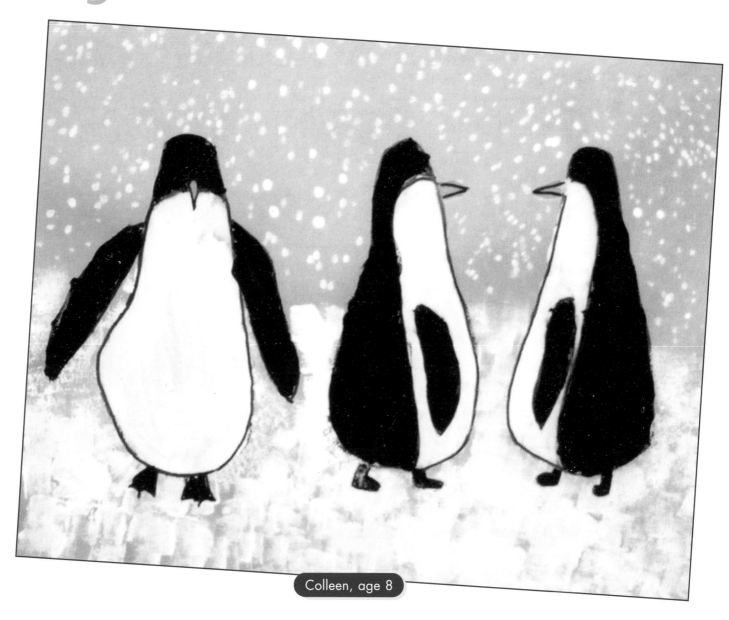

Colleen, age 8

What you need

Old newspaper to protect your work surface

Pencil

Blue or gray construction paper
(12" x 18"/30 x 45 cm)

Scrap paper

Scissors

Black marker

Tempera paints in white, black, and orange

Paintbrushes (large and small)

Container of water and paper towel to clean paintbrushes between colors

Sponge brush (small piece of clean sponge)

Create it with color!

❶ Draw a horizon line across the bottom third of your construction paper to separate the ground from the sky.

❷ Draw a bowling-pin shape on the scrap paper and cut it out. Trace this shape three or four times below the line so that the penguins will look as if they are standing on the ground.

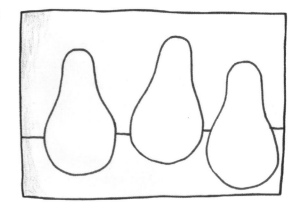

❸ Decide which direction you want each penguin to face and lightly draw in the wings, feet, and faces. Draw a line on each body to show which area will be painted black and which will be painted white.

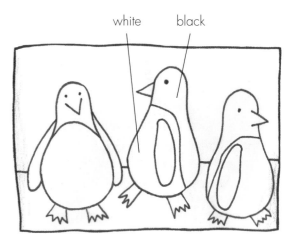

white   black

❹ Outline each penguin with the black marker. Paint the white areas of the penguins. Let dry. Paint the black areas of the penguins. Paint the beaks.

❺ With the sponge brush, dab white paint on the ground to represent ice and snow. Let dry. Use the small paintbrush to make tiny dots of white to represent falling snow.

Black & White & In-Between ✎✎

You might think of gray as a single color, but black and white blended together produce many different gray values (page 78) from light to dark. Experiment with blending black and white to produce a range of this neutral color, then use these grays to produce an intriguing piece of artwork. For another piece of monochromatic (one-color) artwork, see pages 81 to 83.

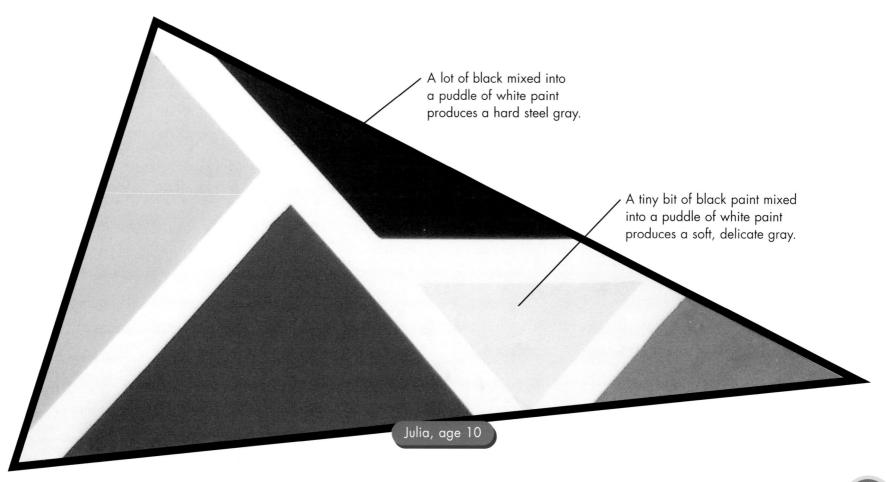

A lot of black mixed into a puddle of white paint produces a hard steel gray.

A tiny bit of black paint mixed into a puddle of white paint produces a soft, delicate gray.

Julia, age 10

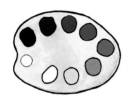

What you need

Old newspaper to protect your work surface

Scissors

Good-quality white paper (12" x 18"/30 x 45 cm)

Masking tape

Paper plates for mixing paints

Tempera paints in black and white

Paintbrush

Container of water and paper towel to clean paintbrush between colors

Glue

Good-quality black paper (12" x 18"/30 x 45 cm)

Ruler

Create it with color!

❶ Cut a large triangle out of the white paper. With the masking tape, divide the triangle shape into smaller triangles as shown.

❷ On a paper plate, mix a very small amount of black into a puddle of white paint to make a very light value of gray. Paint one triangle area with this paint (don't worry if paint gets on the tape).

❸ Mix a little more black into your gray puddle to make a slightly darker value of gray. Paint another triangle section with this mixture.

Think carefully about where to use each value of gray for contrast.

4. Continue making darker values of gray until you have painted all your triangles. Let dry.

5. Carefully remove the tape. Glue your triangle painting to the larger piece of black paper. Trim the paper, leaving a 1/2" (1 cm) black border around your painting.

More Colorful Ideas!

Make a black and white photocopy of a colorful picture. Look at all the gray values and paint a similar picture using different values of gray paint.

"As an artist, I feel color is my most powerful tool. In *Man and Yellow Stripe*, I portray "man" (as in "humans") standing alone in a world of mystery expressed by warm neutral tones of gray. I painted the yellow stripe to symbolize the thoughts and insights that might pass through his mind."
— SKIP LAWRENCE

Man and Yellow Stripe, 2003
Skip Lawrence

Negative Space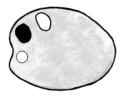

The larger painting of the white flower on the black background provides a whole new way of seeing an object — you create the object by painting the space *around* it.

This concept, called *negative space*, creates a very intriguing image.

This flower is an example of what's called *positive space*. You paint a black image of the flower on the white background. The picture of the flower is there, black and solid.

Jessica, age 11

This painting uses the concept of negative space to show the same flower. You paint the background, leaving the space where the flower would be empty. Think of it like a hole in the middle of your paper!

What you need

Old newspaper to protect your work surface

Paper towel

Pencil

Good-quality white paper

Tempera paint in black

Paintbrush

Where's My Guitar?
Josh, age 10

Create it with color!

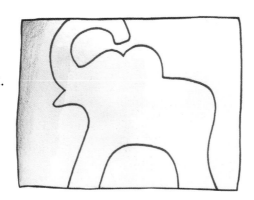

❶ Lightly draw the outline of a flower, an animal, or a musical instrument. Just show the *contours* (the outside edges of the object). Make sure your drawing touches the edge of the paper on at least three sides.

❷ Paint the negative space surrounding your drawing black, revealing the shape of the object.

More Colorful Ideas!

Try painting the negative space around each letter in your name *without* drawing the shape of the letter first. It's easier if you focus on the shapes of the spaces between the letters rather than the letters themselves.

Calico Cat

Known for the markings of different colors of brown on their white fur, calico cats are a fun way to experiment with mixing and using variations of this neutral color.

What you need

Old newspaper to protect your work surface

Pencil

Good-quality paper (12" x 18"/30 x 45 cm)

Tempera paints in red, yellow, blue, and white

Paper plates for mixing paint

Paintbrush

Container of water and paper towel to clean paintbrush between colors

Black marker (optional)

Becky, age 9

Create it with color!

1 Draw a large cat on your paper as shown. Draw a line near the bottom of your paper to represent a rug. See how the cat looks as if it's sitting on the rug?

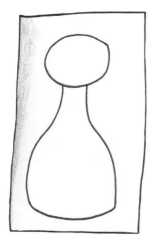

2 Make three variations of brown by mixing different amounts of red, yellow, and blue paint together (page 114). Add small amounts of paint at a time to carefully adjust the colors.

Add a small amount of one brown mixture to a puddle of white to create a tint (page 78). Paint your cat this color.

| brown 1 | brown 2 | brown 3 | tint of brown 1 |

3 Use the other two brown mixtures to make calico spots on your cat. Try lightening one with a little white paint.

4 Paint the rug area with the three primary colors. Let dry. Outline your cat with the black marker, if you want.

Meet the Masters!

Using Art in Color Then

The French painter **Gustave Caillebotte** (GOO-stav KY-bot) used grays and other neutral colors very effectively in *Paris Street; Rainy Day*. Take a look at this large painting on the Art Institute of Chicago's website (RESOURCES, page 125). Painted in 1877, it is considered Caillebotte's masterpiece. From the shiny pavement to the wet umbrellas to the gloomy background skies, Caillebotte uses a range of grays, blacks, and browns to make us feel the dreariness of that damp day.

On with Your Color Adventures!

Well, now you're certainly a color expert! You've used all kinds of colors and color concepts — primary colors, analogous colors, neutrals, tints, and shades, to name a few —to make some amazing art.

But as you've seen throughout in the book, you rarely apply these concepts one at a time. When you're painting, you mix and match color techniques, combining analogous, intermediate, and complementary color ideas, for example, as Kelsey has so effectively done in this jungle scene.

As you choose colors and combine them in your artwork, you can always rely on the color wheel. The position of the colors will guide you in your selection because it will remind you of their relationships. What a great tool!

And while I've given you guidelines for using color in your artwork, remember, that's all they are — guidelines. Real art is about creativity and using lots of imagination. So don't be afraid to experiment and to just plain have fun playing with color. There's a wide world of color out there for you to discover, so enjoy your art adventures!

Jungle Foliage
Kelsey, age 12

Kelsey used tints of blue and green, cool analogous colors, for the background. She mixed several intermediate colors for the jungle foliage. Can you pick out the contrasting complementary colors she used to create interest?

Resources

Viewing Art Online

ArtCyclopedia, www.artcyclopedia.com
A excellent resource for viewing art online; search by artist, name of artwork, or museum location.

Art Museums

While they will never take the place of seeing an actual painting in person, the websites of art museums are nonetheless excellent resources for viewing and learning about artists, specific paintings, and collections. Here are the web addresses of the museums refered to in MEET THE MASTERS! Search for images using either an artist's name or the name of a painting.

The Art Institute of Chicago, Chicago, IL, www.artic.edu/

National Gallery of Art, Washington, DC, www.nga.gov

Solomon R. Guggenheim Museum, New York, NY, www.guggenheim.org/new_york_index.shtml

Virginia Museum of Fine Arts, Richmond, VA, www.vmfa.state.va.us/

Art Supplies

Cheap Joe's Art Stuff
374 Industrial Park Drive
Boone, NC 28607
(800) 227-2788
www.cheapjoes.com

Sax Arts & Crafts
P.O. Box 510710
New Berlin, WI 53151
Phone (800) 558-6696
www.saxarts.com

Dick Blick Art Materials
P.O. Box 1267
Galesburg, IL 61402-1267
Phone (800) 828-4548
www.dickblick.com

Index

Index (cont.)

More Good Books from Williamson

Williamson books are available from your bookseller or directly from Williamson. Please see this page for ordering information or to visit our website. Thank you.

All books are suitable for children ages 7 through 14, and are 128 to 160 pages, 11 x 8½, $12.95, unless otherwise noted.

More Award-Winning Books by Sandi Henry

Parents' Choice Recommended

Orbus Pictus Award for Outstanding Nonfiction

KIDS' ART WORKS!
Creating with Color, Design, Texture & More

Teachers' Choice Award

Dr. Toy Best Vacation Product

CUT-PAPER PLAY!
Dazzling Creations from Construction Paper

Parents' Choice Approved Award

THE KIDS' MULTICULTURAL CRAFT BOOK
35 Crafts from Around the World
by Roberta Gould

Parents' Choice Gold Award
American Bookseller Pick of the Lists

THE KIDS' MULTICULTURAL ART BOOK
Art & Craft Experiences from Around the World
by Alexandra Michaels Terzian

Parents' Choice Recommended
ForeWord Magazine Book of the Year Finalist

PAPER-FOLDING FUN!
50 Awesome Crafts to Weave, Twist & Curl
by Ginger Johnson

The Kids' Book of
INCREDIBLY FUN CRAFTS
by Roberta Gould

Parents' Choice Recommended

The Kids' Guide to Making
SCRAPBOOKS & PHOTO ALBUMS!
How to Collect, Design, Assemble, Decorate
by Laura Check

WORDPLAY CAFE
Cool Codes, Priceless Punzles® & Phantastic Phonetic Phun
Written and illustrated by Michael Kline

Selection of Book-of-the-Month; Scholastic Book Clubs

KIDS COOK!
Fabulous Food for the Whole Family
by Sarah Williamson and Zachary Williamson

Parents' Choice Approved

GREAT GAMES!
Old & New, Indoor/Outdoor, Travel, Board, Ball & Word
by Sam Taggar

Visit Our Website!
To see what's new at Williamson and learn more about specific books, visit our website at:

www.williamsonbooks.com

(This website has books from Williamson Books, an imprint of Ideals Publications.)